P9-EDJ-067

Drama Free

CINDI McMENAMIN

HARVEST HOUSE PUBLISHERS
EUGENE, OREGON

DRAMA FREE

Copyright © 2017 Cindi McMenamin
Published by Harvest House Publishers
Eugene, Oregon 97402
www.harvesthousepublishers.com

ISBN 978-0-7369-6987-1 (pbk.)
ISBN 978-0-7369-6988-8 (eBook)

Library of Congress Cataloging-in-Publication Data
Names: McMenamin, Cindi, 1965- author.
Title: Drama free / Cindi McMenamin.
Description: Eugene, Oregon : Harvest House Publishers, 2017. | Includes
    bibliographical references.
Identifiers: LCCN 2016043271 (print) | LCCN 2017000973 (ebook) | ISBN
    9780736969871 (pbk.) | ISBN 9780736969888 (ebook)
Subjects: LCSH: Emotions—Religious aspects—Christianity. | Peace—Religious
    aspects—Christianity. | Christian women—Religious life.
Classification: LCC BV4597.3 .M435 2017 (print) | LCC BV4597.3 (ebook) | DDC
    248.4—dc23
LC record available at https://lccn.loc.gov/2016043271

Printed in the United States of America

17 18 19 20 21 22 23 24 25 / BP-GL / 10 9 8 7 6 5 4 3 2 1

To the Only One worth making much ado about…

The Shining Star
of the Greatest Story Ever Told—
the Lord Jesus Christ

Acknowledgments

My heartfelt thanks to...

My friend, Connie Boyd, for praying me through the writing of this book, and for sending your insights along the way. You are an encouragement to my heart.

Donna Brown, Cyndie Lester, Allison Martin, Alena Prysch, Rhonda Stoppe, and Barbara Willett, for being real and sharing your personal struggles in this book so others can learn from you how to be drama free. I feel privileged to call each of you my friend.

Chris Castillero, for meeting all the categories in "The Five Friends Every Woman Needs." Your presence in my life is truly a gift.

My daughter, Dana. You were "born for the stage," and your dramatics (which you inherited from your mom and grammy, no doubt) only serve to make you more lovable.

My husband, Hugh, for putting up with me, in spite of the drama.

My Lord, Jesus Christ—the love and inspiration behind my words, my thoughts, and my days. I truly want much more of You and much less of me.

Contents

*The Christian who is truly intimate with Jesus will
never draw attention to himself but will only show the
evidence of a life where Jesus is completely in control.
This is the outcome of allowing Jesus to satisfy every area
of life to its depth. The picture resulting from such a life
is that of the strong, calm balance that our Lord gives to
those who are intimate with Him.*

OSWALD CHAMBERS

*He must become greater and greater,
and I must become less and less.*

JOHN 3:30 NLT

Can We Really Be Drama Free?

I'm no stranger to drama.

I wish that weren't so.

I wish I could tell you that there has *never* been a dramatic day in my life and that I have never, personally, played into drama, contributed to drama, or let drama control my circumstances or responses.

But then I'd be lying to you. And that would be more drama.

The truth is, like you, I know drama. I have lived and breathed it—and even abhorred it—because I live in a world where drama happens. And because I see it in the thousands of women I work among and minister to every year.

It probably doesn't help that I'm a child of a recovering alcoholic, that I'm a "recovering enabler" myself (who just recently figured out what the term *enabler* really means), and that I have been called—on more than one occasion in my life—"dramatic" when all I really want to be is a woman with a gentle, quiet spirit who is pleasing in the sight of the Lord.

I'd much rather be called discerning than dramatic. I'd much rather be considered wise than a woman who occasionally wigs out. And my goal, spiritually, as well as practically, is to become more mature, not more of a mess, the older I get.

Daily I receive e-mails from women who have read my books, or stumbled across my website or an article of mine, asking my advice on how they can manage their lives and be more Spirit led. And as I answer those e-mails, I get the inkling that I just might be in that place where I've finally become a woman whose head governs her heart, who is able to instruct others on how to be more practical than emotional. But at night, as I lie in bed talking to the God who knows me inside and out, I face the sobering reality that I am just as emotionally volatile as you, and I daily need His peace when emotions threaten to overwhelm me.

Oh, how I long to be drama free.

Can you relate to that desire? Maybe your statement is more definitive: "I don't do drama."

I've heard many women say that lately. I've even said it myself. But what does it mean? Are we really saying, "I'm tired of the drama"? "I don't put up with drama"? "From now on, I'm going to avoid drama"? How about: "I'm going to no longer be around a woman who brings me drama"?

As much as you and I would like to shut the chaos, confusion, and cattiness out of our lives and convince ourselves that we "don't do drama," it has a way of creeping into our lives anyway.

Drama happens because life happens. And it happens because emotions are real. Drama happens when unexpected circumstances hit and we are unprepared to handle them. And drama happens when we come up against family members or people with different personalities who carry with them their own sets of emotional baggage, learned behaviors, expectations, values and beliefs, and an ability to misunderstand, misinterpret, exaggerate, gossip, disappoint, and act selfishly and inconsiderately. Just *being around* other people can elicit drama.

Admit it. You've said (or at least thought), *I'm done with the drama...*

...when your mother calls with complaints that you can't help her with. *Sorry!*

...when your teenager is having a meltdown for no apparent reason. *Whaattt?*

...when your coworker blames you for an incident that was clearly not your fault. *Again?!*

...when you get a call from a family member or friend who isn't attending the gathering because *she* is planning to be there. *Whatever.*

...when you discover the talk in the break room, Bible study, or neighborhood has been about you. *Over it!*

...when the woman you confided in betrayed your trust and repeated your story to someone else. *How could she?*

Or maybe—just maybe—someone else has thought *I'm done with the drama* when thinking of *you*.

As I said earlier, I'd like to think I'm never the cause of drama. But in reality, you and I can be catalysts for drama without even realizing it. Yes, *you* have been the cause of drama if you've ever...

...told your friend about another breakup-worthy situation with your boyfriend, yet you can't bear to part with him.

...verbally vented at the customer service rep for how you were treated in the store.

...given another mom a piece of your mind after hearing how her child treated yours.

...said anything about anyone that you wouldn't have said if they were present.

...refused to attend or be involved with something because of another person you didn't want to be around.

...refused to forgive someone because of something they did to you.

...stormed out of a room or meeting (or lost it, emotionally, and then left the room).

Yep, if you've ever done *any* of the above (like I have), then you know drama too. And I'm sure you hate it as much as I do.

Sorting Out the Drama

Not all drama is because we bring it on ourselves. We can be near someone who erupts, or the target of a slanderous campaign, or the victim of a passive-aggressive person who is taking out their frustrations on us. Or sometimes we are broadsided with a diagnosis or a disappointment or a chain of events that has us scrambling to keep our sanity.

....

Whether our drama is the petty stuff or the painful stuff, how we respond makes all the difference in the world.

....

Whether our drama is the petty stuff (like having a bad day or dealing with a website fiasco) or the truly painful stuff that catches us off guard (like a cancer diagnosis, the ending of a friendship, or suddenly losing someone we love), how we respond makes all the difference—or all the drama—in the world.

Assessing Your Drama Factor

Our upbringing, personality, and baggage from past wounds can trigger dramatic reactions to varying degrees, especially if we are unaware of our vulnerabilities and capabilities. Right now, you can assess your own drama factor by answering the following. There are no right or wrong answers, so please don't worry about how you'll score. And don't answer based on the person you'd *like* to be. Be as honest as you can with yourself and answer true (T) or false (F) according to how the statement best describes you most of the time. Here we go...

I don't adapt well to change . . . . T F

I tend to react emotionally to the unexpected and
think more clearly a little later . . . . T F

I've been known to "fly off the handle" at times . . . . T F

I tend to have high expectations of others,
especially those closest to me . . . . T F

I am easily offended . . . . T F

I have a hard time forgiving others . . . . T F

I sometimes tend to think of myself first,
instead of others. . . . . T F

It bothers me when I'm misunderstood
or misrepresented. . . . . T F

I tend to be competitive, especially with other women. . . . T F

I sometimes feel inferior. . . . . T F

I'll do anything to try to help someone. . . . . T F

I have a strong need to be treated fairly. . . . . T F

It bothers me if someone else gets something
I clearly deserved . . . . T F

I can tend to be a controller . . . . T F

I try to avoid confrontation as best I can . . . . T F

I sometimes unknowingly turn a conversation
around so it's about me. . . . . T F

I've been known to tolerate—and even add to—
gossip at times . . . . T F

I like to be a part of solving problems,
even if I'm not asked . . . . T F

I struggle with jealousy at times . . . . T F

I sometimes feel like I need to please everyone . . . . T F

I get frustrated when I can't please everyone
at the same time. . . . . T F

When I want to know something, I have a strong
desire to get the answers immediately. . . . . T F

When I set my mind to something,
I do not want to be deterred. . . . . T F

I have family members who try to pull me
into their problems and issues . . . . T F

I have a hard time staying neutral when it comes
to issues among my extended family . . . . T F

I'm the kind of person who speaks her mind
even when it offends. . . . . T F

I don't mind hurting someone if I'm
speaking the truth . . . . T F

I'd rather stay silent than talk about an issue
that's bothering me. . . . . T F

I care deeply about what others think of me . . . . T F

I expect my husband/child/parent/boyfriend
to fill my emotional tank . . . . T F

I could be classified as a "people pleaser" . . . . T F

I struggle with an addiction (substance, behavioral,
disordered eating, etc.) . . . . T F

Now add up the number of answers you marked true and record the number here: _____. Add up the number of answers you marked false and record the number here: _____.

If you marked most of the statements true, you are most likely one who experiences a lot of drama—either because of the people around you or because of how you respond to life. This book will help you move from a drama-filled life to a drama-free life through learning how to respond to situations and how to walk away from potential flare-ups.

If your answers are pretty balanced between true and false, you seem to have a good handle on the catalysts for drama. Keep reading. This book will be a good affirmation of some of the things you are already doing right, and you'll gain new insights for dealing with areas that still suck you into the drama pit.

If you answered mostly false, you probably picked up this book as a resource for helping other women become more drama free. I'm glad you did. Keep reading. I believe you'll find some insights and application steps that will be helpful for you to share with others.

Now, if you scored pretty high on the drama scale, that isn't necessarily a bad thing. In fact, it means you're pretty much like every other breathing woman on this earth—you have emotions and sometimes struggle with how to express them. But you don't have to stay that way. You and I can learn how to respond, rather than react, to what life brings us so that we can dial down the drama, diffuse it, or eliminate it altogether.

....

We often can't control our circumstances, but we can
always control how we respond to them.

....

We often can't control our circumstances, but we can always control how we respond to them. This book is going to show you how.

Two Kinds, Two Choices

Before we get started, it's helpful to keep in mind that there are two kinds of drama: (1) the drama that life brings (and God allows) and (2) the drama that we create through our response to life.

The drama that life brings is inevitable. Yet how we respond to it determines whether or not it will be fruitful in our lives in conforming us to the image of Christ. Our response to the drama also determines whether God gets the glory or we take the spotlight.

Did you catch that? You and I determine whether the drama in our lives will transform us into more godly people and give glory to God...or shine a spotlight on us and our frailties, insecurities, and emotional instability. Just as God can work all things for good to those who love God and are called according to His purpose (Romans 8:28), so we can take all drama and turn it into a situation that either exalts God or exposes our weaknesses.

Ultimately, we have two choices with every occurrence of drama:

1. We can react emotionally and impulsively and thereby escalate the drama; or

2. We can respond in a reasonable, measured, and godly way and thereby diffuse it and experience peace, joy, and contentment instead.

I know which choice I want to make, don't you?

Let the Show Begin

In this book you will learn how you can begin to make the right choice in every occurrence of drama. In the first four chapters, we'll look at the metaphoric "stages" we perform on, the "script" God has written for us, the role we play, and the other "players" in our story. Then, in chapters 5–8, we'll look at some "scene changers": guidelines on how we can divert the drama when we're hit with unexpected events, when we're overwhelmed, when we're overextended and tired, and when we come up against someone who is self-absorbed. Then in the last two chapters, we'll look at how we can take what we've learned and close the curtain once and for all on the drama in our lives and start living a new opening act that is drama free.

With help from God's Word, plus some practical guidance, I believe you can be drama free—even when the unthinkable happens. Even when you are clearly a victim. Even when life takes an unexpected turn and you are caught in an otherwise overwhelming whirlwind of circumstances that would make any woman lose it. *Even* then.

So come with me as we learn how to pause long enough to realize what we are dealing with, how to better deal with it, *who* we are dealing with, and ultimately Who will deal with it. Then we will be able to diffuse any type of drama that comes our way and replace the chaos with an inner calm.

Inner calm. Do you like the sound of that? I sure do. Inner calm is a quality I want to possess, so I don't start acting like I'm possessed!

So here we go, my friend. Adopt this new motto with me by proclaiming it aloud, and let's start learning how to live it: *As far as it depends on me, I will be drama free!*

Act I

Setting the Scene

All the world's a stage,
And all the men and women merely players;
They have their exits and their entrances,
And one man in his time plays many parts.

WILLIAM SHAKESPEARE

You and I have a choice on this stage God has set us upon. We can either play a small, petty, insignificant role that is all about ourselves. Or we can play a larger, more meaningful role that impacts the lives of others and spotlights the Great Writer of our script. It's all a matter of recognizing Whom we are on the stage to please, accepting the script He has written out for us beforehand, and living carefully and intentionally the role He has designated us to play.

Chapter 1

All the World's a Stage

Recognizing We Already Have an Audience

All the world's a stage,
And all the men and women merely players.
WILLIAM SHAKESPEARE

This is the assigned moment for [Jesus] to move into the center,
while I slip off to the sidelines.
JOHN 3:30 MSG

I'm not proud of this. But I'm going to tell you about it anyway. Several years ago I helped two friends, Scott and Paul, start up a health club about a half hour away from my home. Because I tend to be a take-charge person and I had co-taught a leadership class at my church with Paul, I "unofficially" joined the management team. By "unofficially," I mean neither Scott nor Paul actually *made* me a manager because of the minimal hours I was able to work each week. But I assumed the managerial role anyway. (I also got the nickname "McMinimal" for being the "self-appointed manager with minimal hours.") Scott and Paul often

23

asked my opinion on matters, and the young people we hired began confiding in me and seeking my advice on how to work their way up in the club.

One morning a film crew was in the club to shoot footage for a commercial to run on the local television channel. I wasn't given the details of what we were hoping to convey in the 15 seconds of video footage, but I assumed it would be shots of the personal trainers working with individuals, a row of the shiny new cardio equipment with members enthusiastically working out, and maybe a few seconds of our child-care area, where we had one of the best facilities and programs to offer children while their parents worked out.

As it turned out, the videographers were asked to film a typical day at the club. It wasn't until a few weeks later, when Scott and Paul showed me the commercial that was already airing on local channels, that I saw what "a typical day" was. In one short scene that lasted entirely too long, I flipped my hair around dramatically and quickly walked the length of the front desk area while pointing my finger absurdly in the air as if I was reprimanding someone or chasing them down.

I was horrified at what I saw. It wasn't glamorous. It wasn't even flattering (I've always hated my profile because of the size of my nose!). It was downright embarrassing. Scott and Paul looked at each other, rolled their eyes, and Paul said, "That's a typical day in the club alright…McMinimal pointing her finger and bossing people around."

My jaw dropped open. Is that how my friends and everyone else at the club saw me? *The one who bosses people around?*

They didn't see me as the capable administrator who gave up three days a week of her writing time to help two men start up and run a health club?

They didn't see me as the breath of fresh air to those who came in after a rough day and were greeted by my enthusiasm and warm smile?

They, instead, saw me as "McMinimal—pointing her finger and bossing people around"?

If that was the worst of it, I could laugh off this story and tell it without shame. But after hearing those comments, I sulked the rest of the afternoon and then spent *two days* pouting because I felt my friends didn't see my worth or treat me more respectfully given all the time and effort I had put into their club over the past six months. *Two whole days* of being self-absorbed and overly concerned about how I came across and whether or not I was being valued.

When I returned to work and finally brought up the issue with one of them, he said, "We were joking, Cindi. Get over it!"

And that was the fruit of my two days of pouting—being told it was a joke and I should get over it.

Okay, I did get over it. Eventually. I had no other choice because that's how men typically respond to what they perceive as senseless drama (which I now realize it was). And it was something I learned from.

I not only learned that pouting didn't help my situation any— they didn't retract their words, apologize, or agree to film a new commercial that showed me in a better light—but I also learned another important lesson: All the world is a stage—and we can often make much ado about nothing.

All the world *is* a stage. The place where you work. The home where you live. The store where you shop. The places where you eat. And people are watching (and in some unfortunate cases, even filming), whether you realize it or not.

Whether or not you want an audience, you have it. Whether

or not you want a critique of your actions, it's often there. Whether or not you agree with someone else's review of your behavior or their joke at your expense, it's there, like it or not. And how you and I handle it makes all the difference—or all the drama—in the world.

The Only Player

If my husband had seen that commercial for the health club, he would've jokingly said to me, "All the world's a stage and *you're* the only player."

I once heard him say that at the shopping mall food court about a woman who was making a loud, ridiculous scene and seemed to be enjoying every minute of it. I can't remember the details of the incident. But I do remember his comment and my immediate thought: *I never want that to be said about me.*

And yet, regretfully, I've registered some performances in my life. Not just the ridiculous-looking one in the health club commercial. No, I'm talking about the performances in which I might not have been aware that others were watching my reactions:

- My favorite Target store, where I sometimes think something is on sale but then find out (after it's rung up by the cashier) that the item was in the wrong place and it costs more than I intended to pay.

- The local Chick-fil-A, where I enjoy lunch at least once a week and can never seem to get my "free treat" to scan correctly from my phone app, causing the customers behind me to wait longer to place their order.

- My Jazzercise class, where I can tend to provide too much input and possibly drive others crazy.

- My home, where my family, unfortunately, sees me at my

worst—especially when I'm on a book deadline, or when I've worked all day and then realized I didn't take adequate time to think about my family's dinner plans.

Truth be told, we all have stages upon which we unintentionally perform for all to see and, many times, we are critiqued for that performance without even realizing it. (And I don't think it's exaggerating to say that sometimes we don't get the best reviews.)

Shortly after viewing my embarrassing performance in that health club commercial, I started thinking about my real-life performance resume. What roles have I played, loudly, not realizing who was watching? What amounts of embarrassment have I caused my daughter when I stepped into a role of complainer at a department store, or late and frazzled driver at her school? What types of silent drama might I have contributed to by speaking careless words about another? What behind-the-scenes drama might I have caused others by being unintentionally high-maintenance? And, most importantly, what chance do I have now, at this point in my life, to change my role, rewrite my script, and start being a woman who is drama free rather than drama filled?

The "Stages" of Our Lives

I found it fascinating to read that 75 percent of women in this country suffer from a fear of public speaking.[1] It's called glossophobia. And it's a real thing. I constantly hear women say:

"I don't want to get up in front of people."

"I hate being up on stage."

"Just don't make me give a speech."

"I hate microphones."

I can see the fear in women's eyes and the color fade out of their faces if they think they might have to actually get up on a stage in front of others.

All women *live* on a stage. They just aren't
aware of it most of the time.

And yet 100 percent of women *live* on a stage. They speak unrehearsed lines. They play to audiences. They just aren't aware of it most of the time.

In addition to being on a stage when we're going about life out in the world, we also now have an audience when we are online—in chat rooms and online forums, while posting reviews, and when spouting, posting, or tweeting our political views, personal opinions, and many times inappropriately expressed feelings via social media. Facebook, Twitter, and Instagram (and the dozen or so other social media channels that are out there) have given us even larger platforms upon which we can perform (and also embarrass ourselves). On those "public stages" we have an opportunity to vent without accountability or to shout out what we feel, regardless of how appropriate or inappropriate it might be.

We can stir up more drama by how we fire off a post in response to someone else's because we didn't take the time to stop, think about it, and ask ourselves, *Do I really want to put myself "out there" like this and call attention to myself or my message? Do I really want to say this hurtful, selfish, or demeaning comment?* Or even, *Do I really want to say this meaningless, trite, and ridiculous comment?*

Yes, there's an audience for everything we do, whether we prefer it or not. And although the playwright William Shakespeare penned the words "All the world's a stage...," I believe the Bible has recognized it for centuries by instructing us to please God—our audience of *one*.

In Matthew 6:5-6 (NASB), Jesus addressed the proud human heart that is prone to playing to an audience even when it comes to praying:

> When you pray, you are not to be like the hypocrites; for they love to stand and pray in the synagogues and on the street corners *so that they may be seen by men.* Truly I say to you, they have their reward in full. But you, when you pray, go into your inner room, close your door and pray to your Father who is in secret, and your Father who sees what is done in secret will reward you.

Jesus not only addressed "performance prayers" but the hypocritical habits of the religious leaders of His day who were acting a certain way in public to cover up who they really were in private. He lambasted them for being one way on the outside (while on stage) and another way on the inside (where no one can see):

> Then Jesus said to the crowds and to his disciples, "The teachers of religious law and the Pharisees... don't practice what they teach...Everything they do is for show" (Matthew 23:1-5 NLT).

Jesus then addressed the elaborate pieces of clothing they wore, the way they loved to be the guests of honor at banquets, and the way they ate it up when people addressed them as if they were above everyone else. He called those religious leaders hypocrites because they were on their best "spiritual" behavior on stage but wicked in their hearts and behind closed doors.[2]

Certainly, Jesus knew how tempting it would be for us to put on a good show for others and present a more spiritual image of ourselves in our culture too—or even just an image that is more positive, polished, prosperous, capable, or qualified than we actually are, when God alone knows our true condition. The apostle Paul instructed followers of Christ to serve, perform for, and impress *God*, not others:

> Whatever you do, do your work heartily, as for the Lord *rather than for men*, knowing that from the Lord you will receive the reward of the inheritance. It is the Lord Christ whom you serve (Colossians 3:23-24 NASB).

In 1 Corinthians 6:19, Paul said: "Do you not know that… you are not your own?" Christ purchased His right to us and therefore He can display us wherever He wants.

The often-quoted influential preacher Oswald Chambers wrote:

> There is no such thing as a private life, or a place to hide in this world, for a man or woman who is intimately aware of and shares in the sufferings of Jesus Christ. God divides the private life of His saints and makes it a highway for the world on one hand and for Himself on the other.[3]

Yes, all the world is a stage. What drama are others seeing around you and me? That all depends on what or who it is we fear.

Whom Do You Fear?

It occurred to me as I was reflecting on my embarrassing performances that we create and experience drama because we fear people and not God. We care so deeply what others think of us rather than caring about God's opinion. In his book *When People Are Big and God Is Small*, Edward T. Welch says:

> The desire for the "praise of men" is one of the ways we exalt people above God...Fear of man (and what he thinks of us) is such a part of our human fabric that we should check for a pulse if someone denies it.[4]

....

Fearing *anything other than God* is
likely to trigger drama.

....

The Bible tells us, "The fear of the LORD is the beginning of wisdom" (Psalm 111:10 NASB). I find that verse interesting because I've come to realize the opposite of wisdom is drama. When we exercise wisdom, we use discretion and we don't make a scene. When we display wisdom, we are not putting ourselves on display. If fearing the Lord is the *beginning* of wisdom, which negates drama, then fearing *anything other than God* is likely to trigger drama.

Instead of fearing God, we often fear:

- being misunderstood or misread
- being treated unfairly
- being embarrassed (by appearing weak or incapable)
- being rejected
- being in a situation where we are not in control (My daughter has a fear of flying because she fears not being in

control. And let me tell you, she can be drama on the airplane because of it!)

Sometimes we simply fear the worst. That is still a fear of something *other than God*. It is giving more power to what we fear than to God, who can handle those fears. So much for our overwhelming fear of the stage! It isn't the stage itself we fear. We dread what we will *look like* on that stage and what others will think of us as they observe us being unprepared, scatterbrained, shy, silly, foolish, weak, lazy, or in some way inadequate. Drama is the result of fearing *people* more than we fear God, or fearing circumstances that we believe are more powerful than God. Our fear of insignificance, unworthiness, and rejection also plays a part in our drama.

The Appeal of Drama

My sister-in-law, Sophie, is a wife, mom, and professional choreographer. She has an impressive resume that includes acting, designing and directing dance classes in public and private schools, and running her own dance school, SODE School for the Performing Arts. Sophie offered some interesting insights on why we are attracted to the stage and yet fear it at the same time:

> Drama is expression of emotion and passion to communicate a story. There are ways that this is healing, edifying, emotionally moving, thrilling, and entertaining. But when we bring excessive drama into situations to serve ourselves, the results can be detrimental.
>
> Being overdramatic deflects from the reality of the story that needs to be told. For instance, if I step on a nail on the floor, it causes pain. I sit on the couch, massage my wounded foot, but also warn

someone to pick up the nail so someone else doesn't step on it. I come outside my pain to help someone else, rather than staying in the moment of "I'm so in pain" and not looking out for others within the dramatic moment.

I found Sophie's example insightful. It's easy for you and me, when we are in pain, to be so absorbed in our own drama that we forget about others.

"Many dancers and actors are broken," Sophie said. "They spend their lives working on something to not just be told 'good job' but to be told, 'That was *fantastic*. That was *amazing*. That changed my life.' There is often a deep need to feel special and significant."

She said actors and dancers are hoping for the standing ovation, not just the polite applause. They want the starring role, not just the supporting one. They strive to stand out, be a star, and feel they are worthwhile. In short, Sophie says, "They are looking for validation of who they are."

....

The root cause of our unhealthy drama
is our wounded heart.

....

Is that why we can tend to be dramatic off the stage too? Because we share a deep need to be noticed, to stand out, to be heard, to feel validated and significant? If so, the root cause of our unhealthy drama is our wounded heart.

Have You Been Labeled Dramatic?

Some of us have a dramatic flair and some of us don't. I was raised in a home where we were not taught how to filter or restrain our emotions. So everything was big, loud, and expressive. We talked a lot—and quite loudly! My family was also involved in drama, literally, as my mom directed several high-profile church and community theatrical productions and had my siblings and me on the stage from the time we were young children. So you could say "dramatics" are in my blood. Even my daughter— who has been performing in either dance, vocal performance, or school or community theater since she was four years old— proudly proclaimed to her elementary school teachers and friends of mine that she was "born for the stage" (something my friends didn't let me live down).

But, as dramatic as I can be at times, I've never set out to be high-maintenance or the creator or instigator of drama. And I do believe there's a difference.

Connie (a friend of mine who, unlike me, never learned to express her emotions while growing up) happens to be one of the most easygoing, laid-back women I know. I would think she is as opposite of drama as they come. Yet she lamented to me her surprise when someone called her high-maintenance.

"It crushed my soul," she said. "And recently my husband said I was dramatic, and I had the same socked-in-the-stomach feeling because I never thought of myself as dramatic. I try to be the opposite."

The sting Connie felt is because she associated the word *dramatic* with someone who is "high-maintenance" or "attention-seeking." The dictionary defines *dramatic* as:

- large in degree or scale, and often occurring with surprising suddenness.

- bold, vivid, or strikingly impressive in appearance, color, or effect.

- exciting and intense—characterized, in real life or in art, by the kind of intense and gripping excitement, startling suddenness, or larger-than-life impressiveness associated with drama and the theater.

Okay, so someone who is dramatic is larger than life. That's not such a bad thing.

Awhile back I bit into a fortune cookie after eating my take-out Chinese food, and the little paper strip that I pulled out of the cookie read: "You have a flair for adding a fanciful dimension to any story." My husband laughed aloud and said: "That's Chinese for saying you're dramatic." I smiled and kept that little fortune cookie strip and taped it to my writing desk. That "flair for adding a fanciful dimension to any story" is what makes my sister-in-law, Sophie, a great storyteller. And it's what my friend, Chris, says makes me an interesting writer. People love stories. They love them to be told with expression and dramatic flair. They love to be caught up in the experience. I tend to think I got that dramatic flair from my Father—my *heavenly* Father.

God's Dramatic Flair

God is the most dramatic being I know. The Bible is full of stories that showcase His dramatic flair.

God created the world in six days by simply speaking it into place and then created man by taking a handful of dust and breathing into it. Then He took a rib from the man while he was sleeping and "fashioned into a woman the rib he had taken from the man" (Genesis 2:22 NASB). Now *that* was dramatic flair. God could have, after all, just snapped His fingers and made a man and woman appear or spoken them into existence as He did when He created everything else. But no, He chose to get creative—and dramatic—when He made humans. (And we were made in *His* image—His "dramatic" image! Think about it.)

God chose to start a race of people through the offspring of an elderly couple—a 100-year-old man named Abraham and his 90-year-old, barren wife named Sarah. Why not take a childless couple in their early forties? I mean, really? But God wanted there to be no doubt that He was doing something miraculous. No wonder they called that baby Isaac, meaning, "he laughs." It was dramatic and hilarious (in a beautiful way) all at the same time. Now *that's* dramatic flair.

In Psalm 18, David described God's heroic rescue of him in imagery that is synonymous with dragons in the sky and a thunderous lightning show that splits the mountains. The description of how "smoke rose from his nostrils; consuming fire came from his mouth" (verse 8) and how God "parted the heavens and came down" (verse 9) is the stuff great movies are made of. That dramatic language describes a rather dramatic God.

But there is one common factor in all of God's dramatic flair—it brought Him glory. It showed how big, strong, powerful, and loving God is.

The Dramatic Flair of Jesus

Like Father, like Son, Jesus was dramatic too. We sometimes picture Jesus as low-key, even-keeled, and blending into the crowd. Or sitting stoically on a rock, telling a story softly and in monotone. Are you kidding? He was the Son of God. He was not of this world! He was the creator of the universe confined to flesh and bones. That makes Him far from boring or ordinary. He was the most dramatic human being—fully human and fully God—to walk this earth.

Consider some of the ways Jesus, the Son of God, demonstrated dramatic flair as well:

- He told Peter to go to the lake, throw out his fishing line, and open the mouth of the first fish he caught. There he would find a coin to pay the exact amount of both Jesus' and Peter's taxes (Matthew 17:27). Really? He couldn't just make a coin appear behind Peter's ear like magicians tend to do? Of course He could. But what fun would that be? He wanted it coming from the mouth of a smelly fish. Drama!

- He spit on some dirt, rubbed it in a blind man's eyes, and asked him to walk—dirt in the eyes and all—to a pool and wash it off. When the man obeyed, he regained his sight (John 9:1-11). Only a man with a boyish spirit would want to play in the dirt and perform a miracle with mud!

- He walked out on top of a lake in the middle of a raging storm at night, showing His disciples there was a lot more to fear than merely large waves and some roaring wind (John 6:16-21). (I wonder if He was cracking up inside when they all freaked out and thought He was a ghost!)

- He stripped down to his underwear, got down on the floor, and took on the role of a household servant, washing the dirty, smelly feet of His followers at a dinner in which He was supposed to be the honored guest. He timed this awkward situation at the precise time that His followers had been discussing who among them was the greatest and most spiritual (John 13:1-20). Talk about making a dramatic point!

So tell me, would you call Jesus dramatic? Yet every move He made called attention to His Father in heaven, not Himself. Every miracle He performed, every word He said pointed to the One He came to serve as an example to us of how to follow and obey God. Jesus didn't think for a second about stealing the spotlight or claiming the glory for Himself. He waited until God glorified Him. I believe Jesus recognized that all the world is a stage and His Father in heaven had the sole right to the starring role.

What Are You Proclaiming?

Jesus' dramatic flair was always to show the world who God was and what He could do. But what does *our* drama say to others?

As we express or stuff our emotions, as we interact with others, as we present our views or defend our values, we are broadcasting a message. God's message was consistently I AM. Jesus' message was "I and the Father are one" (John 10:30). But what is the message you and I portray with our dramatic flair?

John the Baptist was probably more aware of the stage than any other person in the New Testament, apart from Jesus. John was like the traveling evangelist of his day. He had an audience everywhere he went. But at one point in his ministry, his followers saw that his audiences were dwindling as more people were starting to follow Jesus and His disciples. John's followers became concerned and asked him about this. His response? "He must increase, but I must decrease" (John 3:30 NASB).

In the New Living Translation, that statement reads: "He must become greater and greater, and I must become less and less." In The Message,[5] that verse reads: "This is the assigned moment for him [Jesus] to move into the center, while I slip off to the sidelines."

Can you and I say that—from the top of the pinnacle when we're experiencing our most successful day, to the lowest point in our lives when our emotions threaten to get the best of us? *He must increase and I must decrease?*

When we can say that, and mean it, we are prepared for any stage in life.

A Point to Process

All the world is a stage, and we have an audience everywhere we go. Every one of us portrays a message by what we say and do.

A Truth to Consider

Fear of man will prove to be a snare,
but whoever trusts in the LORD is kept safe.
PROVERBS 29:25

A Focus for the Week

Think of a practical way you can remind yourself every day this week that you are on stage and God—and others—are taking note of your performance.

A Prayer from the Heart

God, You are the most dramatic being ever. Your dramatic flair captured my heart and inspires me to be all I can be—for Your renown, not mine. Help me to remember that on the various stages in life I have an opportunity to let others see You, high and lifted up— or me, at my very worst. Help me to remember that I have an audience everywhere I go, and in everything I say and do, so that You can be glorified in—and on— every stage of my life.

Chapter 2

Accepting Your Script

Surrendering to God's Greater Story

Man's steps are ordained by the Lord,
How then can man understand his way?
Proverbs 20:24 NASB

I think every one of us can relate to the phrase: *This was not what I expected!*

And if being slammed with unexpected circumstances brings out the drama in all of us, then my friend Donna should be a drama queen by now.

Yet she's not.

Her story makes me wonder how much drama could be alleviated from our lives if we were to immediately take our unexpected circumstances to the One who has written our script. That's what Donna did when she was bombarded with a series of losses over the past four years.

Right after Donna turned 50, her father died of liver cancer. Fifteen months later, her mother was killed suddenly in a car accident. A month after that, her 103-year-old grandmother (with whom she was very close) passed away, followed closely by the passing of her cousin from breast cancer. Then two years later, both Donna and her aunt were diagnosed with breast cancer.

She thought the drama had reached an all-time high with her breast-cancer diagnosis, but two weeks later, an MRI showed cysts on Donna's liver. "When I heard that, fear gripped me," Donna said. "My father died of liver cancer. And I was afraid I would too. I was alone at home when I received that news."

So what did she do? Have a meltdown? Call her friends and cry? Self-medicate? Get in the car and drive to the mall and shop till she dropped?

No. She took her situation to the One who had already written her life's script.

"I hung up the phone and I cried out, 'God, I can't *do* this. I don't want this. I don't want to die of liver cancer. I don't want my boys to be without a mother...But God, I'm *Yours*. Whatever You want of my life, I surrender.'"

That was the extent of her drama. Private. Painful. But short-lived. And toward an audience of One.

In essence, Donna realized her story was bigger than her. And it wasn't about her convenience, happiness, or well-being. It was about Who was ultimately in control of her life and how she could please Him in her surrender. Looking back at that moment, Donna said, "I realized there was no other option for me—I had to surrender or I'd lose my mind."

Donna's MRI showed that the cysts on her liver were non-cancerous. And she believes God, in His grace, used that situation to give her perspective. "Immediately I thought, *As long as I don't have cancer in my liver, I can deal with breast cancer.* I would never have, in a million years, guessed I would've had *any* type of cancer. But suddenly I was thankful for breast cancer. I realized it could be worse."

Within a month, Donna had a mastectomy. A follow-up scan showed that her surgeon had gotten all the cancer and nothing had spread to her lymph nodes or any other part of her body. Again, she was filled with gratitude.

In the midst of Donna's drama of losing close family members and then coming face-to-face with the possibility of losing her own life, she gained a new perspective. "I see absolutely everything differently now," she said. "I don't stress about the small stuff. In fact, I no longer want to live stressed, so I no longer let petty situations affect me."

Trusting God's Script

Strange how the biggest drama of Donna's life pretty much *eliminated* future drama for her because she learned through it to rest in God's plan for her and to not waste another day worrying about meaninglessness. But that's how God works when we acknowledge that He holds our script. And that, my friend, is where peace is found: in accepting—and trusting—God's script for our lives.

....

God knows exactly what He's doing—even when we
think something is spiraling out of control.

....

In Psalm 139:13-16, David the psalmist sang eloquently about the loving writer of our script (and I've added a few thoughts in brackets):

> For you created my inmost being;
> you knit me together in my mother's womb.
> I praise you because I am fearfully and wonderfully
>   made [even in spite of a diagnosis];

your works are wonderful [even those that I don't
   understand],
I know that full well [even when I can't yet see the
   positive side of things].
My frame was not hidden from you
when I was made in the secret place,
when I was woven together in the depths of the earth
   [so nothing got past You].
Your eyes saw my unformed body [including all my
   weaknesses and vulnerabilities];
all the days ordained for me were written in your book
before one of them came to be.

Did you catch those last two lines? *All the days ordained for
you were written in His book* (I like to call it His "script" for our
lives) *before one of them came to be.* God has seen all our days in
front of Him before we've lived out any of them. That means
nothing takes Him by surprise. Nothing is unexpected to Him,
and nothing affects you and me that is outside of His loving plan
for us. The writer, designer, and director of our life's script knows
exactly what He's doing—even when we think something is spiraling out of control.

In Ephesians 2:10, we read: "We are God's handiwork, created in Christ Jesus to do good works, which God prepared
in advance for us to do." There it is again. God prepared good
works *in advance*—before we were ever born and placed into our
life's script.

In a more modern translation, that verse, in the context of the
three verses preceding it, reads like this:

   Now God has us where he wants us, with all the
   time in this world and the next to shower grace and

kindness upon us in Christ Jesus. Saving is all his
idea, and all his work. All we do is trust him enough
to let him do it. It's God's gift from start to finish! We
don't play the major role. If we did, we'd probably
go around bragging that we'd done the whole thing!
No, we neither make nor save ourselves. God does
both the making and saving. He creates each of us
by Christ Jesus to join him in the work he does, the
good work he has gotten ready for us to do, work we
had better be doing (Ephesians 2:7-10 MSG).

When I read words like that, I am in awe that God has a master plan for us. He has given us the privilege of living in close
communion with Him to discover the many amazing facets of
His character, and He has made us the conduit through which
He can accomplish His purposes here on earth.

Through the drama, God is making us more like Jesus.

In Romans 8:28-29 (NLT), we are told what God is doing in
the midst of what we consider unexpected drama in our lives:

We know that God causes everything to work
together for the good of those who love God and are
called according to his purpose for them. For God
knew his people in advance, and he chose them to
become like his Son.

That promise from God assures us that He not only continues working in the script of our lives to make sure we reach His
desired outcome, but He has an overall goal for our story: that we
are conformed to the image of His Son. That, my friend, is why

we sometimes find ourselves in the swirl of unexpected, unfortunate, and unwanted circumstances. Through the drama, God is making us more like Jesus.

Your life is not the small, insignificant story you often believe it to be. Nor is it the huge deal that is all about you that you sometimes make it into. Your life is a story designed by and for your Maker, who wants to glory in His accomplishments in and through you to make you more like His Son. So, the drama that comes your way is designed to change you and transform you into the person He has made you to be. It also means your script is in His hands. And you don't need to panic or fret or pull your hair out when you can't control what's happening.

Understanding God's Transformation Process

Life is full of unforeseen circumstances that God allows to come our way so that we will be shaped into the kind of people He wants us to be. People who:

- live by faith, not by sight. There's nothing like the unexpected to cause us to start trusting God with what we cannot see (Hebrews 11:1).

- depend on Him from day to day. There's nothing like the unexpected to remind us that God is in control and we aren't and we must trust Him (Romans 8:28).

- glorify Him in all things. When others see us lift up God in our circumstances, He is glorified (John 15:8).

Consider how Donna could have turned her unexpected series of losses into personal drama that detracted from God's glory.

Donna could've been angry with God once she started losing people she loved. She could've argued with Him when she saw that the heartache was continuing to happen. She could have crossed her arms, dug in her heels, and said "I'm *done* with this" by the time she got her cancer diagnosis. But what would that have accomplished?

In reflecting on her situation, Donna said: "Sometimes I wonder if I *was* a little angry with God when my mom's accident took place so shortly after my father's sudden death from cancer. I always felt, though, that there was no other option for me but to trust Him. Well, there *was* another option—I could lose my mind! But I choose to trust."

Notice how Donna didn't say, "I *chose* to trust," as if it was a one-time decision in the past. Nope. She recognized that life consists of unexpected circumstances that *continue* to come our way. She realized there could be more losses down the road, more situations concerning her health, more heartbreaks that she may need to cope with this side of heaven. Therefore, Donna said, "I *choose* [present tense] to trust," because it is a daily choice. When we surrender to God's script, we trust His plan from day to day, regardless of whether we agree with it.

In addition, Donna's story could've turned to drama if she had:

- become bitter at God because of all that had been happening around her;
- met with her girlfriends to talk about how life stinks;
- become depressed and chosen to self-medicate or drink to escape her situation; or
- considered only herself and not countless others who are now being impacted and inspired by her story.

Instead, this woman of faith chose to trust that God knows

what is best for her and that He can handle everything she knows she can't.

You and I would spare ourselves much drama if we just learned to trust God's script for us. Life is about more than the here and now. It is about how we will fare in eternity. It's about pleasing our Creator through our submission to His plan. It's about learning what He wants us to learn in the losses and disappointments—and drama—of life.

Throughout the Bible we read of God's transforming process in the lives of people like Abraham, Moses, and Joseph (the favored son of Jacob). Some of these stories start out like tragedies, with one bad thing after another happening. Yet God uses all those unfortunate circumstances to transform the hearts and faith of His leading characters. And in every one of those stories the underlying theme is how big and how loving and how wonderful God is. God is the hero! He saves the day. And He receives the praise and glory—to this day—from the stories in which He brought about amazing results.

Don't think for a second that God is done with that type of intricate work in people's lives today. Scripture says "Jesus Christ is the same yesterday and today and forever" (Hebrews 13:8 NASB). I believe He wants His stories to continue to be told. Not just the ones of long ago that we read about in the Bible, but the ones He is accomplishing today in your life. God wants you telling others of the way He calmed the drama in your life, just as the Gospel writers told others of how He calmed the wind and waves.

It's All About Him

There is one common thread that runs through all the great stories in the Bible: God is glorified. Yet many of those stories could've easily turned into self-glorifying drama on the part of those involved. Take, for example, the story of Jesus' resurrection from the dead.

There was definitely drama the morning Christ rose from the dead. Big-time drama. The most famous individual in Jerusalem (and the whole region for that matter) had just been executed three days earlier by the Romans. The One who fed thousands from a few loaves of bread and a few pieces of fish was now gone. No more free lunches. The One who had stilled the seas for some frightened fishermen and who healed the lame, blind, sick, and deaf was no longer being the medicine man. The One who had actually brought a man back from the dead was now dead Himself. Such drama surrounded the last week of His life and then the public scandal of His crucifixion.

But then the true drama happened. Mary Magdalene, a woman whose life had been dramatically changed when Jesus freed her from demonic possession, went to the tomb along with some other women to apply burial spices to the body of their Lord. But instead of finding His dead body, she encountered drama unlike anything she'd imagined. The stone had been removed from the entrance to the tomb. And Jesus' body wasn't there.

Two angels appeared to the women, asking them why they were looking for the Living One among the dead. They explained Jesus had risen from the dead just as He said He would. Then Mary and the women ran to the disciples and told them everything they had seen. And get this! The disciples "did not believe the women, because their words seemed to them like nonsense" (Luke 24:11-12). So Peter and John ran to the tomb to check it out for themselves.

Now, at this point there could've been drama.

Uh, wait a minute, guys. Do you think we're making this up? We know it sounds dramatic and shocking and absolutely unbelievable, but come on, you've known us for years, and we're not lying or creating drama for a little bit of attention. And we're certainly not delusional!

To any woman, the response of those men would have been rude and insulting.

But did Mary try to prove she was of a right mind and ask the men what motivation she could possibly have to create a story like that? Did she accuse them of thinking so lowly of her that she would stoop to that level to get some attention?

No, Mary didn't give it a second thought. It wasn't about her. It was about her Lord. And He had risen from the dead! When the disciples ran to the tomb to check this out for themselves, I'm sure she was overjoyed.

Run! Faster! See for yourself that He is no longer there!

....

To get over our drama, we have to get over ourselves...

....

I'm so glad Mary didn't take things personally and allow the men's response to get in the way of the greater story God was waiting to reveal. Mary must've realized she was merely a spokesperson for the true star. For you and me to get over our drama, we have to get over ourselves and realize the story is always about Him.

How We Respond

Because of our humanity and sin nature, we have the ability to make any situation or story about us. We are capable of creating drama that isn't there or diverting drama so the focus is on us. Sometimes we do this without even realizing it. In fact, sometimes others will encourage us to focus on ourselves with their well-meaning comments such as, "It's okay, friend. Do what's best for you. You need to think about yourself right now."

Peter, one of Jesus' disciples, tried to comfort Jesus by inadvertently directing Him away from God's plan. And when you look at the story you would think any well-meaning friend would do the same:

> From that time on Jesus began to explain to his disciples that he must go to Jerusalem and suffer many things at the hands of the elders, the chief priests and the teachers of the law, and that he must be killed and on the third day be raised to life.
>
> Peter took him aside and began to rebuke him. "Never, Lord!" he said. "This shall never happen to you!"
>
> Jesus turned and said to Peter, "Get behind me, Satan! You are a stumbling block to me; you do not have in mind the concerns of God, but merely human concerns" (Matthew 16:21-23).

Jesus responded quite dramatically, don't you think?
Get behind me, Satan!
Wow. I always thought that was a rather harsh response from Jesus, since Peter was just trying to help. (Can you imagine calling your friend "Satan" when she is trying to comfort you with her words?) I'm sure Peter felt he was being a true friend by saying, "I don't want that to ever happen to You, Jesus. I love You. And what would I do without You?" Yet Jesus was so aware of the bigger story that He didn't want to get lured into thinking the same thing Peter was suggesting—that He shouldn't have to die. In fact, Jesus rightly recognized that those were the words of Satan, not his well-meaning friend, and so He addressed the source of the statement.

Jesus was well aware of His mission on earth—complete and total surrender to His Father's will, which meant dying to be the

atoning sacrifice for the sins of all who would put their trust in
Him. And when someone, even someone with good intentions,
tried to thwart His purpose, He shut it down.

Now, I believe God ultimately controls what comes our way.
But how we choose to respond determines whether we will grow
through life's circumstances or drown in them.

Notice I said *respond*. Not *react*. We tend to react emotionally
to our circumstances, bringing about unnecessary and sometimes
painful—or at least annoying—drama. But when we respond
appropriately and look for God in our circumstances, we can turn
any situation into a life-changing lesson that molds us and shapes
us into maturity. We will talk more in the next chapter about this.
But for now, let's talk about how we respond to God's script.

A Bad Rap

God gets a bad rap when we don't understand why He
allows—or doesn't allow—something to happen. It's as if we have
a subconscious measuring stick of what we believe a "good God"
would do and allow. The problem with this is that our expectations are skewed by what we think we know about God.

The God of the Bible is so *unlike* you or me or anyone else
we know. And that's the wonder of it all. He is mysterious,
unpredictable, and surprisingly wonderful. And this mysterious,
unpredictable, and dramatic God loves to do the unexpected in
a way that astonishes us and exceeds our expectations. I believe
He loves to surprise us, but unfortunately, we often can't handle
the spontaneity.

God doesn't *need* you to notice Him or acknowledge Him
and give Him credit for the details of your life that He constantly
arranges. He doesn't *need* you to be closer to Him than you are.
His actions are not desperate attempts for your attention. Because
He is God, He *needs* nothing. But He so desires surrender from

you and a deeper relationship with you in which you recognize that He really is God over the universe as well as over the tiny details of your life.

The Real Drama

We looked in the first chapter at how all the world is a stage. But you and I are not the only players. God is in the lead role. He is also the writer of the story, and therefore it is a privilege to be a part of *His* story. We get to play the loved daughter opposite Him as the Compassionate Father. We can be the willing servant opposite Him as the Loving Master. We can be the one in need opposite Him as the Gentle Healer. Yet we so often forget the greater story and start thinking that life is mainly about us and our happiness, our comfort, our disappointment, our problems, our victimization. When we do that, in our minds, we're the only player once again.

God has invited us into this drama in which we will inevitably have days—and sometimes even months or years—of struggling through difficult circumstances. But how we respond to these circumstances and interact with others is the key to the drama factor in our lives. Will we be low-maintenance, moldable women whom God can grow and strengthen through our struggles and inconvenient scenarios? Or will we be women who turn in a selfish, dramatic performance that is all about us?

When we fail to understand that life is all about our Creator and how He wants to be glorified in and through us, we will often develop drama that focuses on us.

Drama Diverted

Have you ever considered that some of the drama in your life could actually be saving you from more dangerous drama somewhere down the road? Because God knows the entire script of your life, He can save you from what you never knew was a threat.

I was reading Psalm 71 recently and highlighted verse 15 in particular, where the psalmist sings:

> My mouth will tell of your righteous deeds,
> of your saving acts all day long—
> though I know not how to relate them all.

I started reflecting on God's "saving acts all day long" and how many I might not even know about. I then started wondering if that is *why* some of the drama happens in my life. Could God be saving me from more dramatic and dangerous circumstances I don't know about?

What do you think? How many times might God have saved you "all day long" and, like the psalmist says, there were too many incidents for you to relate them all? Or maybe you were so caught up in the drama of not getting what you wanted that you failed to see what God had ultimately saved you from? How many times have you recalled yourself saying or thinking:

- "Wow, it looks like that job I really wanted could have turned out to be a disaster. I'm so glad that it didn't work out."

- "Every flight to that destination was canceled—except mine!"

- "If I hadn't forgotten something back at the house, I would've missed that important call."

- "I'm so glad now that he never called back. I may have been spared from a troubled relationship."

- "I was upset that my car wouldn't start that morning,

until I saw on the news about the ten-car pileup on the freeway. I could have been in that accident if I had left the house when I intended."

Yes, the writer of your script may allow unforeseen circumstances to come your way, but instead of freaking out because you're inconvenienced, try thanking Him for the bigger drama that He just might be protecting you from.

Surrender It All

God's great story didn't end when the Bible was finished. It's still being written. He is still in charge. As you surrender to His script, you will find that your own little stage play ceases and you become part of His greater story—a story in which He is the Star and you are the supporting actress. A story in which He is the Hero and you, by God's grace, get to be the heroine. A story that features Him as the Provider and you as the human hands that carry out what He has provided for someone else.

Now that's the story I want to be a part of, don't you?

A Point to Process

You can be drama free when you accept the script God has written for your life.

Two Truths to Consider

We know that God causes everything to work together for the good of those who love God and are called according to his purpose for them. For God knew his people in advance, and he chose them to become like his Son.
ROMANS 8:28-29 NLT

We are God's masterpiece. He has created us anew in Christ Jesus,
so we can do the good things he planned for us long ago.

EPHESIANS 2:10 NLT

A Focus for the Week

Do you know for sure that you are a child of God with a script He has written out for you ahead of time? Although we are all God's creation, we are not all God's *children.* Scripture says each of us is a sinner from the time we are born (Psalm 51:5, Romans 3:23) and we are all, by nature, children of Satan, "the father of lies" (John 8:44). But God found a way to adopt us and make us His own children (Romans 8:14-17). If you are not absolutely sure about your standing with God, you can be cleansed of your sin and receive salvation in Christ (and therefore be considered God's child) when you surrender your heart to Him:

1. Admit you are a sinner by nature and there is nothing you can do on your own to make up for that sin in the eyes of a holy God (Romans 3:23).

2. Accept the sacrifice that God provided—the death of His righteous and sinless Son, Jesus, on the cross on your behalf—in order to bring you into communion with Him.

3. Enter into a love relationship with God, through Jesus, as a response to His love and forgiveness toward you. (For more on developing and maintaining an intimate relationship with God, see my book, *Letting God Meet Your Emotional Needs,* Harvest House Publishers, available at www.StrengthForTheSoul.com.)

4. Surrender to God your right to yourself and acknowledge His right to carry out His plans for you and to mold you, shape you, and transform you for His pleasure.

5. Find a pastor or women's ministry director at a Bible-
   teaching church in your area or a trusted Christian friend
   and tell him or her of your decision to surrender the
   script of your life to Christ. They will want to pray for
   you and get you the support and resources you need to
   grow in your new relationship with Jesus. I too would
   love to know that you have made this decision. (My contact information is in the back of this book.)

Now that you are sure about your standing with God as His
child, highlight an encouraging verse from Scripture in this chapter (or write one down that is a favorite of yours) and keep it with
you at all times so you can read or say it aloud when your life starts
to resemble a tragedy or a drama gone bad.

A Prayer from the Heart

*Lord, I surrender to the script You have for my life. It's
Your script, and I trust what You have planned for me.
Be glorified in and through me. And may all the drama
in my life have but one sole purpose: to lift You up high
so all can see You, not me.*

Chapter 3

Redefining Your Role

Becoming the Woman God Designed You to Be

We can only be used by God after we allow Him to show us the deep, hidden areas of our own character. It is astounding how ignorant we are about ourselves!
Oswald Chambers

I'll admit it. I can be a controller at times. Life is just more comfortable if I'm under the illusion that I'm controlling my circumstances.

I'm not proud of that. The older I become, the more I want to be the *complete opposite* of that. "Controller" is not an attractive label, especially when I'd rather be known as "Spirit-controlled."

I'm glad God wasn't pleased with the "controller" in me either. And I clearly remember the day I learned that it was okay—and actually much more enjoyable—to *not* be in control.

I was returning from speaking at a conference in upstate New York in the fall of 2012 when there was literally a hurricane on my tail. Weather forecasts were saying that the worst storm to hit that area in years was coming fast. I called Hugh and asked him to pray that I'd get home that night because I'd been away for two weeks and I didn't want to be spending the next few days stranded in an East Coast airport.

As I waited to board my plane in Albany, television sets all over the terminal were reporting updates on Superstorm Sandy. The skies were darkening by the moment, and I kept praying.

God, I really want to be home by the end of the evening. I don't even want to think about being stranded here for days. Please, God, You are bigger than this storm. Please get me on this plane and get me home.

Even as I said those words, a knot formed in my stomach. Fear was starting to grip me.

Just let it go, Cindi, I told myself. Or maybe that was God telling me to release what little control I thought I had.

Tears welled up as I surrendered this area of my life that was so hard to let go of.

Lord, I have no control over what's happening right now. And I really wish I did. But You are God, not me. Why is it so hard for me to trust You at times like this? What am I believing about You that isn't true? What am I afraid of? Surely You can still the storm. And surely You can provide for me if You decide not to still the storm. My life is in Your capable hands, God, whatever You decide to do. And please, Lord, rid me of the reservation in me that is afraid to trust You because I fear You will allow the worst. What kind of faith is that anyway?

As I prayed, the truth of Philippians 4:6-7 (NASB) became a reality for me:

> Be anxious for nothing, but in everything by prayer and supplication with thanksgiving let your requests be made known to God. And *the peace of God, which surpasses all comprehension, will guard your hearts and your minds* in Christ Jesus.

The peace that comes through prayer (or maybe it came through my surrender) swept over me. And in that moment I realized God wanted me to be a woman who prays and experiences peace, not one who tries to control and then experiences frustration. Now, for most of my life I've been a woman who prays. But when a worrisome situation happens and my first instinct is to try to control it rather than to rest in the Only One who can control it, then I know God still needs to do a work in me.

As God gave me peace, I became an observer in the airport rather than a worrier. I looked around and noticed others appeared tense. They, too, were dreading news of canceled flights and delayed schedules. I overheard an elderly woman telling a younger couple that she had already been delayed a day on her trip and she was fearful she wouldn't get home in time to take her next dose of medication.

It could be worse, I realized.

Miraculously, I boarded my plane a little earlier than expected, and ten minutes before our scheduled departure, the pilot announced, "It looks like everyone who is supposed to be on this plane is on board, so we're going to depart about ten minutes early. Folks, we've got quite a storm on our tail, and it is my intention to outrun this thing. So I suggest you buckle up, say your prayers, and hope for the best."

With that, we took off. I hit my connecting flight a half hour early, getting me home to San Diego on time, where there was no indication of any type of bad weather (it's okay to hate me momentarily for that statement). As I entered the terminal, the television sets were reporting that the fiercest storm to hit the Atlantic seaboard was shutting down flights all over the East Coast. Several friends and family members called my home that evening, inquiring about my safety. My husband took each call for me and assured them, "Yes, she got out of the area barely in time." We later learned that Hurricane Sandy was the deadliest and most destructive hurricane of the 2012 Atlantic hurricane season, as well as the second costliest hurricane in United States history.[1]

That evening I realized that even Hurricane Sandy couldn't mess with me and my schedule if God wanted to show me what happens when I give everything to Him (and when He's determined to show me that He can control things much better than I can). I slept peacefully that night. Not just because we had outrun that storm and I was home in my own bed, but because there is peace that comes through surrender. And there is relief in knowing we don't have to be the ones to work out all the details of our lives.

That night I dropped the role of "Stressed Girl Who Tries to Control" and let God redefine my role as "Rested Girl Who Leans on the Only One Who Is in Control."

Our Preferred Roles

If we could choose the roles we want to play in life, I wonder how yours and mine might be different than the ones we're living. I suppose we would choose only happy roles, full of blue skies and sunshine, laughter and good health—without pain, problems, or disappointments of any kind. There are two problems with that mentality, however:

1. Those roles aren't available here on earth. They only become available when we reach heaven.

2. If we never experienced storms or struggles in this life, we'd never get the thrill of seeing how God comes through on our behalf and how He changes us in the process.

The here and now is filled with dramatic roles of being molded through our messes, growing stronger through our suffering, and being polished through our pain. My mother is experiencing this now that her role as a wife and woman who has always been cared for is dramatically changing. I asked my Mom to share in her own words the drama that is redefining her role—in her own eyes and God's.

My Mother's Journey

I was confused and anxious about my husband's increasing memory loss. He had seen a neurologist two or three times about his condition, but the doctor never put a name on his diagnosis. I finally asked to see my husband's neurologist privately and began posing my questions. "What do I do when he...? How shall I handle it when...?" The doctor didn't answer any of my questions. He just stood up and asked me to follow him. He led me to a rack of pamphlets describing all sorts of neurological maladies and handed me two and softly said, "I'm sorry."

Dumbfounded, I stuffed the pamphlets in my purse and found my way to the outer office where my husband was waiting. When I finally looked at the pamphlets, I was stunned: *How to Cope with Alzheimer's* and *How Your Local Alzheimer's Association Can Help You*. In fact, I was beyond stunned. I was unable to think or speak. Even after a few days went by, I was still unable to grasp the huge ramifications of that disease.

During the next few weeks, I followed through with the recommended tasks. I contacted the Alzheimer's Association and made an appointment to talk with the director of the local chapter. I cried for two hours while she explained what would likely take place as my husband's disease progressed. It was then that I began to grasp the loss that I would go through. It would be a gradual loss, perhaps similar to a slow death.

I thought I was strong. *The Lord believes I can handle this…therefore, I will.* I talked myself into thinking this would pass, or that I would simply cover up for the times my husband made obvious fumbles or couldn't reason out a simple solution to everyday situations. I would simply take the lead, I thought, and he would learn to follow. *It won't be that bad,* I lied to myself during the daylight hours.

But at night I cried silent tears when I began to think more deeply and to ask God questions. My husband had always taken care of me. I had severe back trouble; I depended upon his help and his wisdom. Who would take care of me? This simply couldn't happen! He was the smart one; I was the creative one. We had been a very unique team in how we served the Lord. There would come a time when neither of us would be able to carry on with the creative projects we were so familiar with. What would we do instead? How would we be able to serve the God we loved? And the tears would flow as I sought God's help and His answers.

I really did believe that God was in charge; I believed that He knew I was capable of handling this, and that somehow, He would make good come out of it for His glory. I believed God knew what He was doing, and therefore, I would go through this with His help. My husband realized he had a problem, but he had no concept of what it meant or what I was going through. For the first time in our marriage, I could not confide in him about my pain. I couldn't count on him to pray for me or for us. He was gradually becoming a stranger, spiritually, and that was taking its toll on me as well. I had always depended on his godly wisdom and strength, and now it was slowly disappearing.

We both attended Alzheimer's group meetings, but I recognized the absence of the acknowledgment of God's sovereignty in the meetings. Everyone was trying to do what they could, and in reality, there was very little anyone could do except to share what they were going through.

About two months into my husband's diagnosis, I was trying to sleep one night and was still begging God to show me how to handle the day-to-day situations. I felt so alone. My husband slept soundly, but I thrashed about, trying to figure out how to cope. I felt like an avalanche was headed for me and I couldn't get out of the way of it, nor bear the weight under it. *Perhaps I would be able to handle this*, I thought, *because God had decided that I could.* But suddenly, I realized I *couldn't* handle this! I was not capable of becoming a caregiver! I had very little patience, and I was the one who needed a caregiver half the time myself. And suddenly the avalanche hit me!

I groaned in agony, rolled out of bed, and stumbled into the living room. I collapsed into a soft chair and began to sob. It was then that I realized that perhaps God had allowed this to come upon us because He knew that I *couldn't* handle it, and therefore, I would have to depend on Him. I think I was even more devastated at recognizing my inability to cope than I was at the situation itself.

When I realized I was unable to cope, I could no longer pray for myself either. I tried to think of someone who could help and minister to me, because I was so pitifully unable to pull myself out of the avalanche that now fully engulfed me. My body trembled uncontrollably, and the tears simply would not stop.

I called my daughter and asked her to pray for me and calm me down. Over the next hour, she prayed for me until I quit trembling and was able to go back to bed.

The next morning, I awoke with a sense of peace I had never felt before! No, the situation had not changed, but the Lord had changed *me*.

At the next Alzheimer's meeting, when the leader called on me to say something, I said, calmly, "I was devastated this week when I realized that I can't possibly cope with my husband's disease. There is hardly anything I can learn or do that will get me through the next several years. But I've turned it completely over to God, and *He* is the only one who can pull me through this. Since I've given up on my own ability to cope, I am confident that God will be the one who will take over this situation. I am totally incapable! And I have found peace in that realization."

The room was quiet. And it remained that way. None of them could cope. But God could!

The disease keeps taking its toll on my husband and on me, but I still have peace. It's not a peace that I might one day learn to cope, but a peace that God will cope for me. He *always* knew that I couldn't handle it.

Where's Your Strength?

Doesn't most drama come from our feeling that we just can't handle the emotional avalanche coming our way? We just can't deal with the situation that is pressing in on us. We just can't be all that people expect us to be.

Yet God doesn't expect you and me to be Superwoman. On the contrary, He wants us to admit how weak and frail we really are apart from Him so that He can be strong on our behalf. He wants to redefine your role—and mine—as a woman who needs Him more than anything or anyone else.

....

God helps those who admit they
can't help themselves.

....

You may have heard the phrase "God helps those who help themselves." But that "verse" is not in the Bible, nor is it even truthful. To the contrary, God helps those who admit they *can't* help themselves.

Scripture is loaded with examples of God calling weak, humble people who not only believed they were inadequate for a task, but actually were, without God's enabling strength. Scripture says that Christ's power is made perfect in our weakness. The apostle Paul told the church at Corinth: "I will boast all the more gladly about my weaknesses, so that Christ's power may rest on me. That is why, for Christ's sake, I delight in weaknesses, in insults, in hardships, in persecutions, in difficulties. *For when I am weak, then I am strong"* (2 Corinthians 12:9-10).

Furthermore, James 4:10 tells us, "Humble yourselves in the presence of the Lord, and He will exalt you" (NASB). If God helped those who helped themselves, that verse would read: "Show yourself capable, and God will come along and help." Many times those of us who believe we can help ourselves don't feel we need God and therefore we don't rely on Him. God wants us to admit we're helpless so we can start depending on *His* strength to get us through situations. That is faith.

Another often-quoted saying that is not scriptural is "God won't give you more than you can handle." The truth is, *God will often give you more than you can handle so that you will depend on Him to carry the load for you.*

The idea that God won't give us more than we can bear may come from 1 Corinthians 10:13, which tells us, "No temptation has overtaken you but such as is common to man; and God is faithful, who will not allow you to be tempted beyond what you are able, but with the temptation will provide the way of escape also, so that you will be able to endure it" (NASB). God will not allow us to be *tempted* beyond what we are able to resist. But He *will* allow us to struggle beyond our capacity in other aspects of life so we understand what it means to surrender and allow Him to carry the burden for us.

God knows our weaknesses and vulnerabilities and wants to be our strength. That's another reason He allows struggles to come our way. Not only does He want to make us more like Christ (as we saw in chapter 2), but He wants us to surrender and say, "I can't deal with this, God, but certainly *You* can."

Reevaluating Your Role

When you are trusting Christ alone for the forgiveness of your sin and for eternal life, you have become His adopted child (John 1:12; Romans 8:14-17). And in that relationship as His child, you have a new identity that does not include the corruption or chaos of your past, or the problems in your present, or the fears of your future. Your drama or problems don't define you either. In your new role, God calls you:

- *His child*—John 1:12 (NASB) says: "As many as received Him, to them He gave the right to become children of God, even to those who believe in His name."

- *His friend*—Jesus said, "No longer do I call you servants, for a servant does not know what his master is doing; but I have called you friends, for all things that I heard from My Father I have made known to you" (John 15:15 NKJV).

- *A saint*—In Ephesians 1:1, believers in Christ are called saints. *Yeah, but I'm not a saint*, you may be thinking. Your actions may not always say it. But your position in Him says it. You are seen as perfect by Him because you are covered in the righteousness and goodness of Christ.

- *Forgiven*—Colossians 1:14 says you have been redeemed (bought back) and forgiven of all your sins—past, present, and future. So your past sins—or your past wounds—can no longer define you. Your slate is wiped clean.

- *Complete*—Do you feel like a "work in progress"? Many women describe themselves this way, referring to how they are not yet what God desires of them. But God's Word is the final authority, and it says "you *are* complete in Him" (Colossians 2:10 NKJV). The work has *already* been done. You just need to live in that truth and wear it.

- *Secure*—You are secure in Him eternally and daily. You are free from condemnation (Romans 8:1-2), free from condemning charges (Romans 8:31-34), and free from the possibility of abandonment (Hebrews 13:5).

- *Unconditionally loved*—Romans 8:35-39 says nothing will be able to separate you from the love of God—not death, life, circumstances, sin, poor choices, a season of rebellion, nothing!

- *His temple*—He lives within you. Your heart is His home. And He dwells with you daily (1 Corinthians 6:19).

- *Royalty*—He says you are seated with Him in the heavenly places (Ephesians 2:6).

- *His masterpiece*—He says you are His "masterpiece," created in Him for good works, which He prepared for you before you were ever born (Ephesians 2:10 NLT).

- *Fully capable by His power*—You are able to accomplish "all things" through Christ who gives you strength (Philippians 4:13 NKJV).

- *His possession*—You are not your own; you belong to Him because you were "bought at a price" (1 Corinthians 6:19-20 NKJV). That means He protects you and provides for you as His own. That also means nothing can touch you that hasn't first gone through His loving hands.[2]

No Longer an Orphan

Do you realize that when we worry and fret and start living a drama-filled life, we are forgetting who we really are? We are, in a sense, starting to live like an orphan.

Oswald Chambers put it this way:

Fill your mind with the thought that God is there. And once your mind is truly filled with that thought, when you experience difficulties, it will be as easy as breathing for you to remember, "My heavenly Father knows all about this." This will be no effort at all, but will be a natural thing for you when difficulties and uncertainties arise. Before you formed this concept of divine control so powerfully in your mind, you used to go from person to person seeking help, but now you go to God about it. Jesus is laying down the rules of conduct for those people who have His spirit, and it works on the following principle: God is my Father, He loves me, and I will never think of anything that He will forget, so why should I worry?[3]

An orphaned child says: "I am all alone. I have no one to help me." A child of God lives confidently the words: "My Father is with me. And He will help me."

....

Live like a loved child of God, not an orphan.

....

The more you reaffirm who you are in Christ, the more your behavior will reflect your true identity—a loved, well-cared-for child of the Most High God. Now, you can refuse to live in your new role, and continue to see yourself in terms of your wounds or your existing drama. Or you can heed my advice: Live like a loved child of God, not an orphan.

No Longer a Victim

Because of our new identity in Christ—which happens at the point of salvation, not through any type of earning this identity—we can live victoriously (and drama free), or we can hold on to remnants of our own small story and live in defeat. The choice is ours.

Do you know what it's like to be around someone who is always the victim? It can be exhausting, can't it? The drama is escalated because there's always a perpetrator, always a conspiracy, always a martyr mentality. When we find life through faith in Christ Jesus, we are no longer victims, but victors. Look at what Scripture says about us, in terms of a victim vs. victor mentality:

- *You are not condemned:* "Therefore, there is now no condemnation for those who are in Christ Jesus, because through Christ Jesus the law of the Spirit who gives life has set you free from the law of sin and death" (Romans 8:1-2).

- *You have God on your side:* "What, then, shall we say in response to these things? If God is for us, who can be against us?" (Romans 8:31).

- *You are more than a conqueror:* "No, in all these things we are more than conquerors through him who loved us" (Romans 8:37).

- *Nothing can separate you from God's love:* "I am convinced that neither death nor life, neither angels nor demons, neither the present nor the future, nor any powers, neither height nor depth, nor anything else in all creation, will be able to separate us from the love of God that is in Christ Jesus our Lord" (Romans 8:38-40).

Those assurances make you and me a victor over (not a victim of) sin. Those assurances mean we have some power in our corner, and we are not powerless. They tell us we are protected and loved, not at the whim of fate or someone else's wrath. Ephesians

1:14 says that in Christ we are guaranteed an inheritance. That, again, makes us not a victim, but an heiress.

Here is a summary of how life looks from the standpoint of a victim or a victor:

The Victim Says...	The Victorious One Says...
That's just my luck.	I am so blessed.
I'm having a bad day.	This is the day the LORD has made, we will rejoice and be glad in it (Psalm 118:24 NKJV).
This only happens to me.	I'm Yours, Lord, for whatever You have in mind.
I'll never be able to do that.	I can do all things through Christ (Philippians 4:13).
I'm a complete failure.	I am a new creation in Christ (2 Corinthians 5:17).

Which sounds more like you? Realize, dear friend, if you find yourself more on the left side of that chart, you have a choice. You can get out of victim mode and start living victoriously through one remedy: praise.

The Praise Principle

Throughout the Bible we read of people who were in a funk and feeling sorry for themselves. There must've been quite a bit of drama going on in their lives, because they were steeped in self-pity. Then, when they started focusing on God and praising Him, their perspective completely changed. For example, in Psalm 13, David cried:

> How long, LORD? Will you forget me forever?
> How long will you hide your face from me?
> How long must I wrestle with my thoughts
> and day after day have sorrow in my heart?
> How long will my enemy triumph over me?
> (verses 1-2)

Poor David. He must've been dealing with some serious drama to feel that God had forgotten him. He was battling negative thoughts in his mind and depression in his heart. So he prayed:

> Look on me and answer, LORD my God.
> Give light to my eyes, or I will sleep in death (verse 3).

David went from being face down in pity to being on his knees in prayer. But look at what happened next. He ended his song up on his feet! Why? He chose to speak praise:

> But I trust in your unfailing love;
> my heart rejoices in your salvation.
> I will sing the LORD's praise,
> for he has been good to me (verses 5-6).

David went from victim to victor through one determined action: praise.

What Kind of Person Are You?

As I said in chapter 2, the key to a drama-free life is making sure we see ourselves as a player in God's greater story, not the star of our own little life. We can best do that by becoming an *explorer* of the person and character of God.

There are basically two kinds of people in the world: the ones who sit back and react to situations, and the ones who move forward and explore them. The ones who react tend to cause drama. The ones who explore tend to avoid or diffuse it. It all depends on how we respond to situations around us. Instead of living in the small, selfish drama of my own little world and reacting, I want to be the woman who experiences the wonders of God's greater story by exploring.

The woman who *reacts* tends to ask, "Where was God?" when something happens that she doesn't like or expect. She complains to her friends, resents how difficult her life has become, and she might even blame God because what He allowed—or didn't allow—was not to her liking.

The woman who *explores*, however, looks for God's presence, His wisdom, His love, and His lessons in *everything*—even situations she doesn't understand. She looks intently at life's circumstances and—in the face of what most would call coincidence—she gives credit to Whom it's due. In the face of life's disappointments, she says, "I don't understand this, but I want to *grow* and know God more through it." There's nowhere for drama to surface in a mature response like that.

Personally, I want to be an explorer when it comes to life's circumstances. I want to be the kind of person who looks for God—and what He wants to reveal about Himself—in everything I encounter.

Staying Calm in the Drama

So what kind of person do you want to be when it comes to responding to the drama in your life?

You and I can choose to respond calmly whether our drama

is little and petty or something big and life changing. We can choose to respond maturely rather than emotionally. Below is an acronym based on the word *calm*. I hope you'll find this helpful whenever drama comes your way:

C—Consider the bigger picture. Life—and therefore every circumstance you encounter—is meant to conform you to the image of Christ. Once you consider this, you can relax and realize God knows what He's doing in the circumstances He's allowing. And you can focus on passing the test rather than failing it through unnecessary drama.

A—Acknowledge God is in control. You are not at the whim of the weather or the most likely predicted outcome. You are not going to consider "averages" or statistics. You are going to trust the God of miracles and whatever He decides to do or not do, for your greater good.

L—Look for the lesson. My lesson in that airplane was that God is bigger than my circumstances and that worry and anxiety are useless. I also looked around and saw many others who needed a smile, a confidence in God, and peace—not a stressed-out woman who couldn't control her emotions. Ask God to show you what He wants you to see in the moment, and then stay tuned to His instruction.

M—Make it a point to praise. In 1 Thessalonians 5:18 we are instructed to be thankful in *all* things, even the unexpected, uncomfortable, and unwanted things. As we thank God for our circumstances—and for whatever He determines to do through them—it will change our perspective and make us people who anticipate His provision rather than dread the worst. That is faith on stage rather than private or public panic.

When drama comes your way, can you apply those steps to stay calm and let God redefine your role from "Scared and

Stressed One" to "Calm and Confident One"? How about letting Him redefine your character from "Fearful One" to "Faithful One"? It's time for you to be victorious over the drama that comes your way and not to be a victim.

Whether you're heading home in an airplane with a hurricane on your tail or heading into an unfamiliar season of life with an avalanche threatening to crush you, be a woman who looks for God in all He is doing through every one of life's circumstances. It is more exciting than you can imagine.

A Point to Process

You can be drama free when you let God redefine your role as a woman who depends on Him to control life rather than trying to control it yourself.

A Truth to Consider

*I am confident of this very thing, that He who began a good work
in you will perfect it until the day of Christ Jesus.*
PHILIPPIANS 1:6 NASB

A Focus for the Week

What is one word (or phrase) that you would hope others would use to describe you?

_____

Now, what can you do every day this week to reinforce that description of you, no matter what stage you are on?

A Prayer from the Heart

Lord, I truly want to be the woman You have designed me to be. Oh, to be more like Your Son, Christ Jesus. Yet life's drama so often gets in the way. Help me to stay calm in the midst of the chaos so I can truly experience Your peace and pass that on to others who so desperately need it.

Chapter 4

Casting the Players

Surrounding Yourself with Strong Women

The righteous choose their friends carefully,
but the way of the wicked leads them astray.
PROVERBS 12:26

Do not be misled: "Bad company corrupts good character."
1 CORINTHIANS 15:33

I remember meeting the Drama Queen at the first church where my husband served as the senior pastor. I was only 27 years old, pregnant with my first child, and a little intimidated to be the pastor's wife in a church where every person was older than me.

One of the women in the congregation introduced herself to me by excusing her obnoxious behavior: "I'm Carrie [not her real name, of course]. You'll get to know me real soon. I'm the one who always says what I think."

Hmmm. I decided right then and there to keep a safe distance from Carrie.

It didn't help though. I still knew exactly what Carrie thought of me. On the occasions she didn't tell me directly, she told someone else what was wrong with me:

- My newborn daughter was "too fat" because I was "overfeeding" her. (How do you do that when you're breastfeeding, anyway?)
- My skirts were too short for my long legs.
- I had "more shoes than Imelda Marcos." (For those of you who don't know who she was, that's fine. It was a gross exaggeration anyway!)
- I was avoiding the congregation because I didn't like them.

I think that last one hurt the most because I really *did* like the congregation, but our first several months at the church I was not only working full time (four ten-hour days with a two-hour round-trip commute) because we couldn't live on my husband's salary alone in such a small church, but I was also struggling with morning, afternoon, *and* evening sickness on account of being pregnant. When I wasn't working, I was home in bed feeling lousy!

As a young pastor's wife, those criticisms crushed my heart. I wish Carrie had told me a few of the things I was doing right, or even just told me directly what she felt I was doing wrong. I could've grown through that situation in learning how to handle confrontation. Yet she smiled at me to my face and sneered at me behind my back.

It's a good thing that church also had a faithful member named Helen. Helen was a lot older than Carrie. Helen was also an encourager. Not a Sunday went by that she didn't give me a warm smile, compliment me on something, and offer some helpful words such as, "We've all been there, sweetie, don't you worry about a thing," when my brand-new baby was fussy and I didn't know how to keep her quiet during the service. Helen always let me know she was praying for me. I can't help but think she was aware of Carrie's tactics, too, because she always seemed to be there with an encouraging word on the heels of a Carrie encounter. How could I not love Helen? How could I not want to be just like her one day? I appointed her as my only child's honorary great-grandmother. And to this day I have not forgotten her sweet smile and her timely words of wisdom and encouragement.

Helen was a good antidote for the drama of Carrie.

Checks and Balances

Do you have some checks and balances in your social circle? Do you have a friend or mentor like Helen whom you can count on to say the right thing at the right time when the office Drama Queen is spewing her venom that could easily set you off? Or when your neighborhood "Carrie" is spouting off careless words that eventually find their way back to you?

Maybe you are acquainted with a few women who can be gossips or drama queens now and then. Scripture tells us "bad company ruins good morals" (1 Corinthians 15:33 NASB). Bad company also leads to drama. Sometimes we can't get away from that bad company, but we can clearly choose our friends.

Christian women often get the idea that they must be friends with everyone.

Christian women often get the idea that they must be friends with everyone. Yet the Bible tells us, "A man of *too many* friends *comes* to ruin" (Proverbs 18:24 NASB). I believe that's because when we try to be friends with everyone, we can't be loyal to anyone.

Scripture also tells us, "As iron sharpens iron, so one person sharpens another" (Proverbs 27:17). I'm a person who needs to be sharpened and challenged. I also need to be refreshed, warned, advised, encouraged, and understood. There's a lot that I need in a friend. There's also a lot I need to *be* as a friend.

Sometimes you and I don't actually *choose* our friends—they just find us, and before we know it, we're hanging out with someone who is either helpful or a hindrance. However, Scripture tells us "the righteous choose their friends carefully" (Proverbs 12:26). If you and I want to dial down the drama in our lives, it would be wise to take inventory of our friendships.

The Five Friends Every Woman Needs

I recently came up with a list of the five types of friends I need in my life. I then shared it with some moms, who then shared it with their daughters, who then shared it with their friends. Eventually the list was published, and it's now used as a resource for mothers as well as women who want to be balanced in their friendships. As you read through this list (which is not in any particular order), you might want to highlight the kinds of friends you currently have to get an idea of how balanced you are. You might also use this list as a guide for praying about the friendships you might still need.

1. *The Fun Friend.* Let's admit it. We *all* need someone who is fun to be with—who makes us laugh and encourages us to set the work aside, have some fun, and live a little. You and I can't spend every waking moment with this friend, because if we did, we'd never get anything done. But if you have a friend who can balance the fun with

responsibility and maturity, and encourage you to let go of work now and then and not take yourself so seriously, you have found a treasure. *Who encourages you to not take yourself so seriously?*

2. *The Firm Friend.* I'm not talking about the woman who is constantly working out and has considerably less body fat than the rest of us. Although you and I need *her* too (we'll get to her later), we need a friend who will firmly tell us what we *need* to hear, not just what we *want* to hear. While your fun friend may encourage you to laugh it off or live for the moment, your firm friend will often remind you of what's best for you, even if it isn't fun or even comfortable. She does this because of her love for you and her ability to see beyond the moment to what really matters. And if she's able to be firm with a generous dose of grace and love, hold on to her. She is a rare gift. *Who tells you what you need to hear instead of just what you want to hear?*

3. *The Forward-Moving Friend.* You've seen her. You probably even admire her (or maybe you can't stand her because she seems to have it all together!). She gets excited about New Year's resolutions and seeks out people to join her in them each January. She talks about what she's reading, what she's learning in her Bible study, or the latest class she's taking to explore something new. Do you have someone to challenge you to be healthier, to read more books, to think more deeply, to hone your skills? We all need to keep moving forward personally, emotionally, physically, and spiritually. *Who challenges you to move beyond where you are right now?*

4. *The Faithful Friend.* Every woman needs a friend who

will be there through thick and thin. Through the dark days, through the sick days, through the days you are having difficulty and just need someone to understand. Not only is the faithful friend always there, but she's loyal—meaning she would never talk behind your back or reevaluate the friendship if she thinks she's giving more than you are. A faithful friend doesn't keep track of how many times she has called you versus how many times you have taken the initiative to call her. She will pick up with you wherever the two of you left off. The opposite of the faithful friend is the gossip or critic. Proverbs 16:28 says, "A whisperer separates the best of friends" (NKJV). Your faithful friend is the one who will never be whispering to others about you. *On whom can you always depend, regardless of season or schedule?*

5. *The Faith-Filled Friend.* Do you tend to be a worrier? Do you stress out when a situation seems out of control? If you hang around others who do the same, you will fuel each other's fire of fear and doubt. That's why every woman needs a faith-filled friend who doesn't worry or talk about the "what ifs" but trusts in the Lord and helps fill up others with her faith. When your concerns cross the line into worry, doubt, and fear, that's when you need your faith-filled friend to remind you Who is ultimately in control.

Your faith-filled friend also fills your tank and leaves you feeling more energized and stronger by being in her presence. This world is filled with drainers who empty us through cynicism, complaining, and gossip. But a faith-filled friend will build you up with her attitude and perspective. She is also quick to forgive and is the opposite of the angry or bitter woman who holds on to offenses and drags others down by the issues in her life. Proverbs 22:24 tells us not to befriend the bitter woman: "Do not make friends with a hot-tempered person, do not associate with one easily angered." Instead, we are to surround ourselves with others who can sharpen our faith and fill our tanks. *Who strengthens your faith when it's faltering, and who fills your tank when you're running on empty?*

The older I get, the more I find that true friends are few and far between. If you have at least one friend in each category above (or all the categories are covered by the few friends you have), you are rich beyond measure. And if there's a friend on that list whom you don't yet have, you know what to look for…and the kind of friend to *be* as well.

People Who Are Potential Drama

While you may have certain friends who come to mind as you look at that list, there may also be some friends or acquaintances you need to limit your time with in order to have less drama in your life.

Avoidance isn't the answer. But erecting boundaries around your time, limiting your social activities with these women, and sometimes just keeping a safe distance helps. These are the women you want to have less of in order to dial down the drama:

1. *The Gossip.* Proverbs 20:19 tells us, "A gossip betrays a confidence; so avoid anyone who talks too much." If you are around a woman who is gossiping about another woman, the chances are pretty good she will gossip about you as well. It's also difficult to avoid joining in when you are around someone who gossips. So limit your time around women who talk about others.

2. *The Exploder.* Have you ever been around a hot-tempered person, one who is known to explode or vent easily? If so, you have probably learned to tread lightly. And yet, must we constantly walk on eggshells around people who are emotionally volatile? The Bible is full of warnings to stay away from hot-tempered people. Proverbs 29:22 tells us, "An angry person stirs up conflict, and a hot-tempered person commits many sins." Proverbs 15:18 says, "A hot-tempered person stirs up conflict." And we are exhorted to be around people who hold their tongues (Proverbs 11:12; 13:3), not those who explode all over us and others. Proverbs 21:23 warns, "Those who guard their mouths and their tongues keep themselves from calamity." When we stay away from the woman who doesn't know how to guard her mouth, we spare ourselves much drama.

3. *The Stuffer.* This person quite possibly never learned to express her feelings or emotions, or she was taught to stuff them inside. The problem is, after stuffing for too long, she is bound to implode. Or explode. On you. Some of your friends may be stuffers who just feel more comfortable not talking about what bothers them. But that leads to tension. And tension means drama. Communication is vital to healthy relationships. Passive-aggressive people tend to stuff it all in, but that never ends well. If you have a good friend who is a stuffer, encourage her to talk to you about how she feels, and affirm to her that what she expresses is safe with you.

4. *The Cynic.* We all know one. Or two. Or several. At times, we can be one of them too. Especially if we hang out with them. Cynics are those who see the glass as

half-empty instead of half-full. They are the ones who let
you know the downside of every situation and the ten
reasons why your great idea is a bad one. They are always
waiting for the other shoe to drop, or they are the ones
who are actually throwing it on the floor! These people will be the first to tell you why you can't achieve that
dream, or get that job, or trust God to come through.
Proverbs 22:10 says, "Drive out the mocker, and out
goes strife; quarrels and insults are ended."

5. *The Victim.* In chapter 3, we looked at the differences
between a victim and a victor. How exhausting it is to
be around the perpetual victim! She always has a sad
tale. Everyone is out to get her. If you live with or must
be around the victim, heap on the gratitude, praise, and
positive comments to be a sharp contrast to the misery
in her life. It might make her sick of you (misery loves
company and tends to resent the sunshine), but that way,
everyone else isn't sick of *her.* Praise not only changes
your perspective but it might change hers too.

6. *The Needy Woman.* She exists everywhere and tends to
cling. She starts out sincerely wanting a friend, but then
she needs so much of you that you find you can't give
anymore. While believers are to sincerely help those in
need when prompted by the Holy Spirit, we need discernment about befriending and hanging out with
women who need so much from us. The person your
needy friend really needs is Jesus, and by always being
there for her and always trying to meet her need, you
deprive her of an encounter with God that may transform her life and make her dependent on Him alone.
Don't let the needy woman drain you and bring drama

to your life. Instead, point her to Jesus—the only one who can meet her emotional needs. (If you have a needy friend, you may want to gift her with my book *Letting God Meet Your Emotional Needs*, which will help her depend more on God and less on you.[1])

Terri, a reader of my blog and books, told me she is no stranger to the needy woman:

> I remember my pastor telling me once that my kind heart was a good quality, but it would also result in me getting hurt a lot by other people. Since I always wanted to help people and would seek out ways to get involved in my neighborhood, at work, or at church, I wouldn't always have the best discernment about the women who befriended me or needed help. They would appear one way and suck me in with the friendship I craved, but eventually I ended up getting hurt each time and the relationship would end. As I got older, I learned to put a guard up about who I let into my life.

All of us need to be guarded when it comes to our time, investments, and relationships so that we don't become women who enable others and add drama to our life—and theirs.

Don't Be an Enabler

I have a natural tendency to enable. One reason is because I grew up in the home of an alcoholic. When you are surrounded by those with addictions, it's natural to want to cover it up and excuse the behavior. However, by doing so, we enable the addict to continue his or her harmful behavior.

It's always been difficult for me to discern the difference

between enabling someone and being Christlike toward them. Isn't serving someone enabling them? And Christ called us to serve others. Isn't loving them unconditionally enabling them? And Christ calls us to love and forgive others unconditionally. I didn't understand the difference until I took a good look at Jesus in Scripture. Jesus did not enable others to continue in their sin or dysfunction. He empowered them to change.

....

Jesus did not enable others to continue in their sin or dysfunction. He empowered them to change.

....

Enabling someone's rude, inconsiderate, or dysfunctional behavior is not loving. Enabling is not synonymous with patience and other fruits of the Spirit. Enabling a person's bad or unhealthy behavior is ignoring the issue and allowing them to continue it. Enabling always leads to drama, which can result from pent-up anger and bitterness.

The only drama Jesus participated in was the dramatic glorification of His Father. In John 13:1-20, when His disciples argued about who was the greatest, Jesus didn't placate them. Instead, He launched into a memorable (and humiliating) lesson on servanthood by taking off his outer robe, grabbing a towel and a basin, and washing their dirty, grungy feet. Jesus, the God-man, who was a billion times more worthy than all twelve of those guys combined, took on the role of a household servant and washed *their* feet. Jesus did for those men what they should have already thought to do for Him. Instead, they were more concerned about which one of them was the most worthy!

My friend Brenda, a mom and minister to others, reminded me of something about Jesus' character when it came to not being an enabler: "Christ often drew the attention of a lot of people as He moved about in ministry, and we have several examples of times when the people left once their emotional or physical needs were met (or sometimes unmet). It's interesting to me that He never sought to chase them down (enabling drama). Instead, He left them to go their own way, even telling His disciples at one time to shake the dust off their sandals and move on to the next town. In some ways, this is a great visual for us when we encounter drama."

Brenda is right. Some women want help when it comes to the drama in their lives, but others don't. So don't chase them down. Some women want to vent, but you don't always need to be the one to hear it. Some people want to bring others down; don't be the one they pull down. Others want a partner in crime or complaining. Don't volunteer.

Don't Be a Drama Instigator

Do you walk into the room and improve the scene or add drama?

I love how Henry Blackaby, in his book *Holiness*, suggests that we bring a presence of God with us everywhere we go. He says we need to be a highway through which others can become more holy.[2] I want to be a highway to holiness in other people's lives, not a detour to drama.

Here's how you and I can do that:

1. *Hang with God First.* There's only one who can purify our hearts and make us the kind of people who can refresh others rather than instigate drama. Sitting with God and seeking Him first on a matter will also give us wisdom to know how to handle a situation. Go to Him first and let Him calm your anxious heart.

Terri says, "Drama increases in my life when I take things too seriously, and this often happens if I haven't been praying consistently or in the Word of God much. As the drama increases, then depression, fear, and panic will try to overtake me. That's why it's so important I spend time with Him first."

2. *Have a Mentor.* Do you meet regularly with a woman who can help you stay grounded spiritually and cultivate a heart and life that is pleasing to the Lord?

My friend Peggy Sue says,

> I meet with a mentor who hugely helps me step back from hurt, expectations, and drama and align my heart and thoughts with God's. When my relationship is focused vertically on God first, then He brings peace and the security I need and guides me to love others through Him. It's a triangle with me at the bottom left, God at the top, and others at the bottom right. When I strive to have a relationship going from me to others along the bottom line of left to right, drama is not far behind. When I have a relationship with God that goes from my left corner up to God at the top, and then down to others as I relate to others through God first, drama is diffused.

3. *Raise Your Standards on Who You Share Your Time With.* On the surface, this might sound snobbish. But there is only so much of you to go around, and so many others who might want or demand your time. That amounts to drama. You want to spend your priority time with your priority people—the people who will cry the most at your funeral (not the most dramatic ones, but the ones who loved you, and the ones you loved the most).

Therefore, choose to be around positive people who lift you up, sharpen you, make you better, and who pour into you. In my book *When You're Running on Empty*, I stressed the importance of keeping good company and how it can keep you from feeling drained. I also laid out some principles for keeping yourself positive, which includes limiting your relationship to builders, not drainers. Although having no drainers in your life sometimes isn't possible (especially if they are present in your own family, church, or workplace), you can choose whom you let into your life the majority of the time. Focus on those who are positive and drama free.

Pray for Discernment

As I've mentioned before, how we respond to our circumstances can determine whether or not they turn into drama. But when it comes to friendships, we can, in some ways, choose our circumstances by choosing the people with whom we spend the majority of our time. God brings some people into our lives to refine us and expose the raw areas that He still needs to work on. And He brings others into our sphere of influence so we can minister to them. Pray that God will give you the discernment to know the difference between His divine appointments and women who are simply drama and need to be given a smaller role on the stage of your life.

A Point to Process

You can be more drama free when you focus on friendships that encourage and challenge you, both personally and spiritually, rather than drain your time and energy.

A Truth to Consider

Drive out the mocker, and out goes strife;
quarrels and insults are ended.
PROVERBS 22:10

A Focus for the Week

Pick up the phone and call or write a note to each friend who fills one or more of the areas in the list of "The Five Friends Every Woman Needs" on pages 82–85. If you have a friend who meets *all* of those areas, reinforce to her how grateful you are that she is in your life. Then ask God to make *you* that kind of friend as well.

A Prayer from the Heart

Thank You, Lord, for the friends You have given me who build me up and encourage me to be all I can be for Your glory. Please give me discernment about who should have the bulk of my time and how to limit my time with those who simply add drama to my life. May I be to those drama-filled people a breath of fresh air and an inspiration of how to live for You rather than myself.

Act II

Changing the Scene

We really can eliminate the drama in our own lives
and diffuse it in the lives of others around us.

Walk through these four scene changers with me
and learn practical ways to avoid the meltdown, find
your center, and experience peace when you're feeling
overwhelmed, overextended, or as if you're about to
blow!

Chapter 5

Scene Change–
No Longer Overreacting

Developing Strategies for the Unexpected

*Like a city whose walls are broken through
is a person who lacks self-control.*
PROVERBS 25:28

*D*rama happens when the unexpected occurs—if we don't
have a strategy for dealing with it.

Allison learned this when her two sons were young.

Now, I've been told that moms of boys know what it's like to
be in and out of the emergency room and constantly dealing with
the unexpected. In fact, as one mom of boys told me, "We should
expect the unexpected when we raise boys."

But nothing prepared Allison for the day her son Kyle nearly
broke his neck.

Kyle was almost six years old when he jumped his bike off
the neighbor's driveway, a six-foot-high embankment, and fell

onto his head on the sidewalk below. His helmet smashed upon impact, and his bike fell on top of him after he hit the ground.

"I ran toward him, panicked," Allison recalled. "I remember thinking he'd broken his neck since he landed facedown and his helmet was smashed. As I approached, he got up and kicked the bike off of him because he was so mad that he fell. I yelled, 'Don't move, lie still!' But he was flailing around, and it was clear he had broken both his arms.

"I carried him into the house, trying to stay calm—and keep *him* calm—and tried to call my husband. Three times I dialed the wrong number!" Allison left a message for her husband to meet her at the hospital and then immediately got Kyle to the emergency room.

Kyle had two broken arms, a goose egg on his head, and a split chin. The doctor took a look at Kyle's goose egg and said, "He should've been wearing a helmet."

"He *was* wearing a helmet," Allison said, explaining that it had been smashed upon impact. The doctor replied: "I'm glad, or we would've been at a children's hospital dealing with a whole different set of issues."

When Allison's husband, Guy, arrived at the hospital, Allison was all drama.

"You should've seen his helmet—it was all smashed up. He could've been *killed!*"

"But he wasn't," Guy said.

"He could've broken his neck, Guy! He could've been paralyzed!" Allison insisted.

"But he isn't," Guy said again, calmly.

Still hysterical, Allison said, "You don't understand; he could've *died!*"

"But he *didn't*, Allison," Guy said firmly, but softly.

Suddenly, she got it.

"I stopped my panicking and realized Guy was right. My son didn't break his neck. He wasn't paralyzed. He didn't die. So why keep going on and on about what *could've* happened?"

Looking back at that incident, Allison says, "My husband has been my best example of how to be drama free."

Learning New Responses

For a while, I believed the myth that women are more emotional than men. Maybe because I've seen more women lose it emotionally in public than men. But recent studies debunk that notion and conclude that men feel emotions just as deeply as women. Our childhood experiences, personality, and learned responses all contribute to how we *express* our emotions. But whether you tend to fall apart emotionally when handling the unexpected, or silently stuff your feelings for an eruption at a much later date, you can learn new responses that are healthier and more productive.

Allison explained that Guy is an engineer, and through his job of supervising the design and manufacture of products, he has learned how to respond to life's variables that women often refer to as drama. "Guy has to work through problems on his job," Allison said. "There always has to be a strategy as they make products, otherwise they keep missing things. If you make a product, it's not always going to work. So Guy's team has to develop problem-solving skills that consider all the variables and provide solutions each step of the way. It gives them a framework for solving problems."

She believes that the way Guy approaches work and the products he makes is the same way she needs to approach life. "We worry when we don't see the light or the truth or a way through a problem. My husband has taught me that, just like on his job, life is a situation where there are variables, and there constantly has to be a strategy."

Developing a strategy for problem-solving has helped Allison through the years—not only in raising two active sons, but in her former position as a women's ministry director at a large church and now as she continues to mentor women—including myself—through the variables of life.

A Strategy for the Unexpected

Drama is the result of reacting emotionally without a plan.

When the unexpected comes your way—through an accident, a disaster in your home, or a sudden turn of events that leaves you broadsided—you need to have a plan. Drama is, after all, the result of reacting emotionally without a plan. Your plan might be as simple as praying first and responding second, so that your response is less emotional and more practical. Here are some strategies to consider so that you will be prepared:

Be a Problem Solver

In the case of Kyle's accident, a dramatic reaction, assumptions, blame, or predictions of what could've happened weren't helping. Allison had to work the problem:

1. Get him to the doctor.

2. Find out his condition.

3. Take the next steps to help him recover.

"When we don't know how to problem-solve, we panic

instead. And that is drama," Allison said. "Some things we can't change. But we can focus on how we got there. When we learn from a circumstance, we can get ourselves out of it. For instance, in Guy's work, his team must continually ask, 'What are the circumstances that affect us? What got us here? What are our options for fixing this?'

"It helps me to write things down so they don't seem so over-whelming or vague," Allison said. "Then it's in black and white, and it looks like something I'm able to tackle. A counselor once told me to take each decision and run it to its logical conclusion. What does it look like in one year, five years, ten years?"

Be Flexible as Circumstances Change

Having a plan isn't enough. That plan might need to change. And when we are unable or unwilling to adapt to change, there is more drama. That's why we need to be flexible.

Allison said she was once told by a labor-and-delivery nurse that the pregnant women who came in ready to deliver, clutching tightly to their birth plans, often didn't fare as well as those who were flexible and ready to adapt to change. Nothing ever goes exactly as planned with the delivery of a child. There are so many variables, thus the need for constant adaptation.

It's the same with life. There are a million variables, and those clutching tightly to their "perfect life plan," who are unwilling to adapt to change, will experience more drama than those who are flexible and take life as it comes.

"Don't be the Cinderella trying to have the fairy-tale ending," Allison said. "Instead, look at reality as well. Sit with God in it awhile and be open to a new plan as He reveals it."

Be Focused on the Truth, Not the What-Ifs

If Allison had focused on the fact that her son was relatively unscathed after his fall, she would've experienced and exhibited far less drama and been able to start working the problem. Philippians 4:8-9 (NASB) offers us this advice:

> Whatever is true, whatever is honorable, whatever is right, whatever is pure, whatever is lovely, whatever is of good repute, if there is any excellence and if anything worthy of praise, dwell on these things…and the God of peace will be with you.

Did you catch the first three words in that passage? *Whatever is true.* Scripture commands us to focus on the facts of the situation, not our feelings.

Allison was focused on the possibility that her son could've been killed, but in fact he wasn't. You and I may feel that our situation is out of control, but in fact God is *in* control.

When we look at what Philippians 4:8-9 exhorts us to focus on, we have to take into consideration each one of the attributes, not just one or two. Allison pointed out: "If we focus on just what is true, we will still worry if that truth looks bleak at the moment. We then have to focus on what is honorable and right." Those instructions to focus on what is true, honorable, right, pure, lovely, and of good repute can be summarized in this way: *Focus on the character of Christ.* He is truth. He is honorable. He is right. He is pure, lovely, and of good repute. He is excellent and praiseworthy, and He is able to give you inner peace in the midst of the panic.

Be Balanced with Wisdom from the Word

So often we need direction. Even when God is guiding us, we get frustrated when we can't see what He's doing.

"Drama is like being willy-nilly tossed back and forth. We need discipline to balance ourselves out," Allison said. James

1:5-6 tells us we can find that balance when we ask God for wisdom. But we aren't to ask for it halfheartedly, with panic in our hearts. Instead, Scripture commands us to "ask in faith without any doubting, for the one who doubts is like the surf of the sea, driven and tossed by the wind" (NASB). You can be anchored, emotionally, when you are seeking God's wisdom and peace in every situation. Even by just praying instead of worrying, you are ushering peace into your life (Philippians 4:6-7).

Overreacting to Offenses

When it comes to not overreacting, it's not enough to have a strategy for dealing with unexpected events and accidents. We also need a strategy for how to deal with the unexpected *offenses* in life—the personal accusations, misunderstandings, careless words, and sometimes unintentional actions on the part of others that rub us the wrong way.

In her years of ministry, Allison said she's seen a common reason for drama—especially among followers of Christ. "The spirit of offense is what causes division between people," she said. "It's what splits churches." The Scriptures say, "For our struggle is not against flesh and blood, but against the rulers, against the authorities, against the powers of this dark world and against the spiritual forces of evil in the heavenly realms" (Ephesians 6:12). So we must recognize that either the enemy is stirring up the drama to divide God's people, or our own flesh is having its way, which is causing dissension.

Consider how the typical "spirit of offense scenario" causes drama:

1. You are hurt.
2. You refuse to talk to the person who has hurt you. Or, worse yet...

3. You share your wound with another person who then sides with you and also alienates the person who hurt you.

In the case of either number 2 or 3 above (or both), drama occurs.

The more we examine Scripture, the more we find that a Spirit-controlled person is not one to give in to the spirit of offense. Proverbs 19:11 says, "A person's wisdom yields patience; it is to one's glory to overlook an offense."

Galatians 5:19-21 (NASB) lists the characteristics of a person who is *not* under the Holy Spirit's control:

> Now the deeds of the flesh are evident, which are: immorality, impurity, sensuality, idolatry, sorcery, enmities, strife, jealousy, outbursts of anger, disputes, dissensions, factions, envying, drunkenness, carousing, and things like these, of which I forewarn you, just as I have forewarned you, that those who practice such things will not inherit the kingdom of God.

Wow, if that isn't a description of drama, I don't know what is! At first glance, you and I might think, *I don't do any of that!* And yet when I looked at that same passage in the New Living Translation, several words stood out to me as causes or effects of our inability to deal with the spirit of offense:

- hostility (enmities)
- quarreling (strife)
- jealousy
- outbursts of anger
- selfish ambition (disputes)

- dissension

- division (factions)

- envy

The next two verses describe the characteristics of a person who is controlled by the Spirit of God. Notice how all these characteristics stand in contrast to the list above:

> The fruit of the Spirit is love, joy, peace, patience, kindness, goodness, faithfulness, gentleness, self-control; against such things there is no law (Galatians 5:22-23 NASB).

Do you realize that by possessing just *one* of the fruits of the Spirit in the list above, you would be able to blow off the spirit of offense? It doesn't even matter which one, because if you focused on love alone, it would deter all those elements of drama. If you focused solely on self-control, it would definitely diffuse your contribution to drama. If you focused on patience or gentleness or kindness, any of those character traits would diffuse drama. But the wonderful result of being under the Holy Spirit's control is that when you surrender to His leading, you get *all* of those characteristics of God's Spirit, not just one or two.

....

The more Spirit-filled we are, the less
drama-filled we will be.

....

How much overreacting would you and I do if we were *filled* with love, joy, peace, patience, kindness, goodness, faithfulness, gentleness, and self-control? Clearly the more Spirit-filled we are, the less drama-filled we will be. And to be Spirit-filled simply means to be Spirit-controlled, yielding to Christ's controlling Spirit in us, not our fleshly impulsiveness.

Strategies for Dealing with the Spirit of Offense

Allison said, "I once worked with a woman who would let everything steamroll her. She'd get so off track. She let everyone else's opinions get to her. It taught me something. If there's drama, it usually goes back to, 'This person said that about me and I was hurt.'"

We can't control what others say or think about us, but we can control how we respond. More importantly, it's helpful to remember that, as Christians, we live for an audience of one—God Himself.

If we truly know that God's opinion of us is the only one that matters, we will be able to do the following when offended:

Realize There Is Always More to the Story

Much of our offense comes from having too little information. There is always another side to the story. There is always a context within which the story—or the offensive statement or action—occurred. And there is always a backstory (what a person may have been dealing with that caused her to say or do what she did to offend you). Ask God for the discernment to know if you really need to hear the context or the other side of the story, or if you need to just let it go. Get in the practice of taking every offense to God and asking Him to show you what, if anything, is true in the accusation or offense, and what to release so you can move on.

Retain a Sense of Humor

When we retain a sense of humor, it keeps us from taking ourselves—and our offenses—too seriously. I experienced this after speaking at a retreat one weekend. My book table assistant had to leave early, and I found myself alone while helping a line of women who were waiting to purchase books from my table before heading home.

One woman who waited rather impatiently finally got to the front of the line and, after I apologized profusely for her having to wait so long, she made a few snappy comments that I didn't understand. When I asked for clarification, she said, "Just take my money and give me my [expletive] books before I change my mind and storm out of here. There are so many things that are not going right today." Taken aback, I asked if I could be a listening ear or pray for her, and she looked at me in disbelief and said sternly, "I'm going to tell you *one more time*—take my credit card, give me my books, and I'm outta here." I couldn't resist the urge to hand her (in addition to the two books she bought) a copy of my book *Women on the Edge*, and I said, "You better take this one too as a gift from me, because you really need it!"

I don't think I've ever had that quick of a comeback for someone who caught me off guard. But I had to laugh as I said it to her, hoping my humor would lighten the situation. Two women standing next to her—whose jaws dropped open when she spewed her anger at me—immediately smiled, and one of them chuckled out loud. As the drama queen left, the other two women apologized to me on behalf of her attitude and said they really hoped she would read that book because she definitely *was* a woman on the edge and had been for quite some time.

During my drive home, I asked God to soften her heart and be her comfort and peace with whatever was causing her pain that weekend. I also asked the Lord to show me what I could learn from that encounter and how to better respond to situations like that in the future. When I got home, I was greeted by an e-mail from her, apologizing for her brash behavior and thanking me for

Women on the Edge. She admitted that she needed it, that it was the book she *should've* bought. I responded graciously, and she responded back with a few smiley faces, showing me her ability to laugh at the situation as I had. Humor can often help ease a dramatic situation—especially if there's some prayer involved too.

Refrain from Acting Impulsively

Being impulsive in our words and actions often leads to drama. James 1:19 tells us, "Everyone should be quick to listen, slow to speak and slow to become angry."

Oswald Chambers said:

> Impulsiveness is a trait of the natural life, and our Lord always ignores it, because it hinders the development of the life of a disciple. Watch how the Spirit of God gives a sense of restraint to impulsiveness, suddenly bringing us a feeling of self-conscious foolishness, which makes us instantly want to vindicate ourselves. Impulsiveness is all right in a child, but is disastrous in a man or woman—an impulsive adult is always a spoiled person. Impulsiveness needs to be trained into intuition through discipline.[1]

Resist the Urge to Defend Yourself

This step has been the most helpful to me through the years. I can lose sleep at night trying to defend my image, or waste energy on explanations, defenses, or attempted retaliation. But none of that is necessary when I realize one golden truth: God's got my back.

There is such freedom in being able to let an offense or accusation fall by the wayside with the mindset, "My name is Christ's.

Therefore an accusation against me is an accusation against Him. And He can defend His name."

There is such freedom in being able to let an offense or accusation fall by the wayside.

I love the advice that author Richard Foster gives in his book *Celebration of Discipline*. He says this about the discipline of silence:

> A frantic stream of words flows from us because we are in a constant process of adjusting our public image. We fear so deeply what we think other people see in us that we talk in order to straighten out their understanding.

But, Foster says, when we choose to be silent—putting the "stopper on all self-justification"—we are showing God and others that we believe He can care for us, reputation and all.[2]

Remain Hidden

A woman who is drama is one whose first love is herself and who gets easily offended by what others say or think about her. I want to be a woman who pays no regard to what others think of me because my identity and reputation is wrapped up and hidden in Christ.

The Bible tells us:

> Therefore if you have been raised up with Christ, keep seeking the things above, where Christ is, seated at the right hand of God. Set your mind on

the things above, not on the things that are on earth. For you have died and your life is *hidden with Christ in God* (Colossians 3:1-3 NASB).

As I'm writing this chapter, I am experiencing a little of what it means to be "hidden." Just eight months after an expensive redesign, my website went down this week, leaving me virtually invisible. There is no way, at the moment, for meeting planners to find out about my ministry and book me for their event. Readers of my books or online articles won't be able to find my "hub." For all they'll know, I've vanished.

It occurred to me, while this was happening, that perhaps that's what we should be in the midst of drama: invisible, so others see Christ and not us. Imagine, as you are being offended, as people are talking about you, as someone is going out of their way to make you miserable, if you were to just stay "hidden with Christ in God." Because your life is hidden in Him, He is protecting you and guarding your name, which is really *His* name. By hiding yourself in Him, you can stay hidden until He works it all out. (You certainly couldn't escalate drama in that condition, could you?) And as God takes care of His own, the perpetrator of drama would have nowhere to go with it. You would be unresponsive, invisible, hidden with Christ in God.

Oh, to be so invisible that I diffuse any drama that comes my way.

To be hidden with Christ is to identify with Him so completely that we don't care about our image or reputation anymore. It is a form of complete surrender. I believe we don't like the idea of complete surrender because we think it means we are giving God permission to take us through something difficult.

But life *is* difficult. And God doesn't need our permission for anything He desires to bring into our lives. Jesus said we will have trouble in this world (John 16:33). It's not just a biblical cliché. And yet, as Allison's husband often reminds her, "None of us is getting out of this alive." We all die before we leave this earth.

Therefore, adjust to the changes, the disappointments, the unexpected twists and turns in life. Allow them to lead you to a greater dependence on the Lord. As you do that, you'll experience the best kind of drama—the dramatic way in which you will grow in your relationship with—and dependence on—God!

A Point to Process

A strategy can help us remain drama free when hit with an unexpected circumstance or offense.

Three Truths to Consider

The LORD will fight for you; you need only to be still.
EXODUS 14:14

"No weapon forged against you will prevail, and you will refute every tongue that accuses you. This is the heritage of the servants of the LORD, and this is their vindication from me," declares the LORD.
ISAIAH 54:17

Fools show their annoyance at once,
but the prudent overlook an insult.
PROVERBS 12:16

A Focus for the Week

There are five steps in the "Strategy for Dealing with an Offense" on pages 106–111. Choose one to focus on each day of the week and repeat a couple on the weekend. In time you will become a woman who is responding maturely rather than over-reacting, no matter what comes your way.

A Prayer from the Heart

Lord, forgive me for the times I've overreacted to my circumstances or to an accusation made against me. That kind of response sadly shows You and the world that I believe I'm on my own and have to fend for myself. But You've got my back, Lord, in every situation I encounter and every offense that I perceive. Help me to trust You with caring for me, reputation and all.

Chapter 6

Scene Change—
No Longer Overwhelmed

Finding Your Center

They cried out to the LORD *in their trouble,*
and he brought them out of their distress.
He stilled the storm to a whisper;
the waves of the sea were hushed.
They were glad when it grew calm,
and he guided them to their desired haven.
PSALM 107:28-30

[Wisdom's] ways are pleasant ways, and all her paths are peace.
PROVERBS 3:17

arbara is a spiritual mentor to me. From the time I first met this lovely pastor's wife, I was drawn to her dramatic flair. I think it was her passion for God, for her husband, for her ministry, and for the just cause of others that made me think of her as dramatic. But this girl spoke my language. And I couldn't help but fall in love with her personality and her heart for God.

Through the years, we've kept in touch and seen each other often. She's been a loyal reader of my books (and often a contributor) and has probably heard me speak more than anyone else. (She proudly refers to herself as a "Cindi Groupie.") She's one of the most grounded women, spiritually and emotionally, that I know. I've never imagined her as the type to fall apart.

And she never imagined she'd be in a place where she nearly would were it not for Jesus.

This morning Barbara e-mailed me. I'd been asking for her insights on how women can diffuse drama in their lives. I knew with all she had been through in the past few months, she'd have some real-life advice for real-live women who experience real-live drama.

She started her e-mail, though, asking for "friend grace."

"I must withdraw from the project," she wrote. And then she explained all that was going on that morning and revealed, without realizing it, who and what it is that keeps her drama free:

> I just returned from my mother's place, where I found her lying on the floor at 9 a.m. She had spent the whole night there. She fell, bruised her face, bit her lip, and is now not able to stand up nor balance herself. I'm making calls for help, contacting facilities, and taking care of her until this all comes together. I left her in bed and will be dashing back soon.
>
> I have your questionnaire on my desktop. I started to see if I could contribute regarding past discipleship experiences, my own experiences, and now care-giving for my mother, but I'm dry. I have nothing to give. I looked at each question and nothing came to mind, but with all this going on right now today, I can reflect on how I feel right now…

What I realized is I have chosen, over this past year, to make sure I do not turn the events in my life into drama. Quieter and calmer on the exterior isn't what I've been able to achieve, but I know how to get to that place out of necessity or I'd lose my mind. Because, as the events of life mount, that's how you feel—like your head will explode. Like you just wish the Lord would take you. Truly. No joke. There are days there is no motivation, no delight.

Having my mother diagnosed with dementia and moving her near me to help with her care was just the start of it. Add to that getting a breast cancer diagnosis, surgery, awkward and annoying healing, and a pending reconstruction surgery. I'm dealing with knowing that it will be six months to a year before I have something visually as to what the new me will look like; add oncology, blood tests, and appointments every six months for five years—all this coupled with the day-to-day responsibilities of life and me wanting to go to the gym. Will I *ever* get to the gym? What about me?

And just as her e-mail started to sound like drama, she found her center.

Taking every thought captive to Christ is a Scripture we toss around, and yet it is exactly what we have to do to eliminate the drama in our lives and keep our sanity. I need to take every—every—thought captive. At times like this, every thought is varied and comes like a machine gun assault. So it's not easy; it makes you weary. But it's what He offers you to make sense of it all, to put things in order. *God is a God of*

order, so I focus on that one thing. What is the order
so I can get the most important thing moved along
and not sit frozen? In reality, I don't want to do anything at all, but I have to.

So I stay in this hour, writing to you. I can't think
of the past hour because that's where regret is. I can't
think of the next hour because that's where hopelessness resides. But this hour, writing to you, all is well. I
liken it to being on a freeway lane and, distracted, I
run over the lane bumps; my stomach turns over, I
grab the steering wheel, and I get back to center. All
good. Ahhhh.

Even as Barbara wrote to me, she was guiding herself back to
what she knows of her God, the One she can trust and hope in
today.

I guess that word *center* appeared off my fingertips
for a reason. It caused me to think of the center of
His love, protection, and comfort. Being able to
cry out, complain, and pout from the center of His
love makes me feel like I'm being held. I think of
being five years old and I just don't want to do any of
this. And then He pulls me close and assures me I'm
going to be okay.

I hear the drama in what I'm writing, don't you?
But it's all inside my head, where He and I can handle it. Because frankly, that's where He makes sense
of it all. Bypassing Him and becoming a heroine in
the one-act play I can write and rewrite and rewrite
accomplishes nothing. Sure, I share thoughts with
my husband and daughter and siblings, but typically that's when I've got it sorted out with Jesus

first. Notice I didn't say, "That's after I have it *solved* with Jesus." It's just sorted so I can go to Him again and say: "You know how I was doing great yesterday? Well, today I'm dying inside. I don't expect You to fix this, but want You to know this is hard. All this is hard—the cancer, the mother, the finances, the chores, everything, and no time for me."

When Barbara was diagnosed with breast cancer, she remained drama free, she said, because she "hunkered down and kept the information, research, appointments, and decisions close."

My initial tests and results I went to alone because I knew I couldn't add another person's emotions to what I had going on in my head and heart. And I'm not talking about advice, care, concern. I mean riding in the car and hearing comments about inane things, critiquing other drivers. I needed to claim inward peace. I had healing Scriptures on my playlist in the car and in my ears while waiting to see doctors, and by my bed at night when I'd wake up and start to think. My thoughts are roaming, wanting to solve, trying to figure out the unknowns, needing the truth of the Word playing over and over to calm the chaos in my mind.

It was me and Him. He knew what the results were, I trusted Him, I didn't regret anything in my life, and I didn't feel like I needed to be around for anything, like seeing my granddaughter walk down the aisle. As time went on, meeting with surgeons (general and reconstruction), researching endlessly, participating in the process, watching the video of breast tissue removal, I realized something about myself. I wanted to be in the game when I was under the anesthesia. I realized I had an issue with the unknown and the enemy, and my flesh ignited a spirit of fear. It was anxiety of the unknown that I was experiencing, which is all about control, right? And, therefore, it was all about surrender.

Barbara said she has never felt discriminated against—or like a victim—in her cancer diagnosis and in having to care for her mother.

I never say, "Why me, Lord?" Because I know He'd just say, "Why not you?" What I say to Him is, "I don't want to." And He says, "You and I can do it together," and I go to that place again where God is a God of order. What is out of order in my thinking? Let's get this back in order. I need to get to that hour, that center where I feel calm and claim the joy for all the blessings. He's given me such good things in my life even if only as basic as a roof over our heads, food, stage-one cancer and not stage four, the sweetness of my mother going through this, and how she must feel.

Yes, take every thought captive to Christ, exchange it for thoughts of holiness and joy and try my best to have a good sense of humor and a great attitude because this "ain't no joke," none of it. It's hard and sad and scary, but it's the walk He knew I'd be walking, and He's on it with me.

After reading Barbara's e-mail, I cried. What is my drama in the scope of what she's dealing with? How bad is it, really, for me to feel the hurt of an untrue accusation? Or to feel the pain of neglect from a friend I haven't heard from in months? And how insignificant my fear seems now of not being able to pay my bills at the end of the month.

I'm sure, at times, Barbara believes her drama is nothing in the scope of something more serious that she is made aware of in someone else's life. And yet God knows what overwhelms each one of us. And He is there, as our center, putting things in order and helping us sort it out.

Staying Centered

Barbara mentioned two actions that have helped her find and keep her center:

1. Capture your thoughts
2. Correct your thinking

Let's take a closer look at how we can stay centered.

Capture Your Thoughts

The verse Barbara quoted about taking our thoughts captive is found in 2 Corinthians 10. There, we are instructed to take our thoughts captive to the obedience of Christ because we are in a spiritual war in which the enemy will do his best to run rampant through our thought life, creating doubt, fear, chaos, and confusion. Here is that verse in context:

> Though we live in the world, we do not wage war as the world does. The weapons we fight with are not the weapons of the world. On the contrary, they have divine power to demolish strongholds. We demolish arguments and every pretension that sets itself up

against the knowledge of God, and we take captive
every thought to make it obedient to Christ (verses
3-5).

Do you realize that when you feel overwhelmed by health
problems, or too many commitments, or relationship difficulties, or emotional distress, it's possible the enemy of your soul has
already formed a stronghold within you and is having a heyday
with your thought life? Your only defense is to take those mis-
directed thoughts captive to the obedience of Christ so they are
not running loose in your head and wreaking havoc with your
emotional state.

Taking our thoughts captive to the obedience of Christ means
capturing or binding them with the truth of God's Word. The
process looks like this:

Loose Thoughts	Captured Thoughts
I can't get through this situation.	I can do all things through Christ (Philippians 4:13).
I'm alone in this.	Christ has said He'll never leave me (Hebrews 13:5).
I'm being punished by God.	There is no condemnation for those in Christ (Romans 8:1).
I've blown it and there's no chance for me.	I'm a new person with a clean slate (2 Corinthians 5:17).

This will surely overwhelm me.	He will be with me through floods and the fires (Isaiah 43:2).
I won't be able to make ends meet.	My God will meet all my needs (Philippians 4:19).
The worst I can imagine will surely happen.	God will work this according to His best (Romans 8:28-29).

....

The more we know of God's Word, the better we will
be able to tame our reckless, wild thoughts.

....

As you looked at that chart, did you notice how taking your thoughts captive to the obedience of Christ involves Scripture? The more we know of God's Word, the better we will be able to tame our reckless, wild thoughts. That leads me to the second point in Barbara's strategy for finding her center:

Correct Your Thinking

Years ago I heard a Christian counselor say that when women begin to feel overwhelmed by life and start to freak out, she asks them, "What are you believing about God that isn't true?"

I can't get through this, you may think. But what are you believing about God that isn't true? Are you believing that He has abandoned you? Are you believing that He is no longer good and will no longer be your help? Are you believing that you are at the whim of your circumstances and, therefore, God is not, in fact, in control?

If you've read any of my previous books, you will remember this phrase: Focus on the facts, not your feelings. What are the facts about God when your feelings are telling you otherwise? When our feelings lead us down a dark tunnel of despair, we need to switch on the facts of what we know about God to direct us back out.

When we know Who God is and what He is capable of, our worries, fears, and freak-outs can be stilled.

I love the biblical account of Jesus calming the storm when the disciples started having major drama. (And they say only women experience drama!) In Luke 8:22-25 we read what happened:

> One day Jesus said to his disciples, "Let us go over to the other side of the lake." So they got into a boat and set out. As they sailed, he fell asleep. A squall came down on the lake, so that the boat was being swamped, and they were in great danger.
>
> The disciples went and woke him, saying, "Master, Master, we're going to drown!"
>
> He got up and rebuked the wind and the raging waters; the storm subsided, and all was calm. "Where is your faith?" he asked his disciples.
>
> In fear and amazement they asked one another, "Who is this? He commands even the winds and the water, and they obey him."

Now, I've never been out on a boat at sea during a storm. I imagine if I was, I would be just as scared as Jesus' followers. But I have experienced various personal storms that left me momentarily doubting, frightened, and fearful that I'd been left to my own devices.

During one such storm, a friend told me to remember where

Jesus was when the disciples were being tossed by the waves. He was right there in the boat with them. And He was able to get them safely to the other side.

....

> If Jesus can still the wind and the waves,
> certainly He can still my frenzied emotions.

....

When an emotional storm hits me, when I'm being rocked about by the winds of fear and the waves of worry, I remind myself that I should be as if I'm asleep in the bottom of the boat, confident that Jesus will get me to where I need to be. After all, if Jesus can still the wind and the waves, certainly He can still my frenzied emotions. If He can calm the violent seas, He can calm His trembling child. He is a God of order, and He has everything under control.

Debbie's Dilemma

Debbie had to remember this when she found herself overwhelmed by a series of unexpected events in her grown sons' lives. She wrote to me and told me where she ultimately found her center:

> As a mom, I had always put every ounce of my energy into raising my boys. Now 21 and 28, it seems youth was an easier experience. You'd think if I can get them to adulthood everything will be great. Well, five years ago the unexpected happened and we had a grandson on the way with no wedding. We rallied as a family, and my son and his girlfriend produced two children without being married. Then, my son's girlfriend walked out of our lives, stating

she had not had enough freedom and wanted neither motherhood nor the role of a wife.

I now have a son who is the single parent of two boys. Talk about stress and drama! My other son had to be hospitalized for four days for depression three years ago, and my husband decided after many years of being an absent father and husband (he was there physically, but always chasing after other dreams and people) that he also wanted another life because life at our house wasn't fun anymore.

I was crushed and began having panic attacks and anxiety. I had never known what a panic attack was until now. I had put everything into my marriage and excused the bad behavior by my husband, thinking if I could only make everything perfect enough, with no stress for him, he would love me and we would one day be fine. My sons reaped the benefits from me and the failures of us both.

I have learned to walk every day in faith and when it becomes too much, I reach out to my few mentors who are strong Christian women for support, comfort, and encouragement. I reach for the Bible and sometimes still let my emotions take over, but I always come back to the foundation of God and His Word. Some nights I fight through an anxiety attack while hanging on to my Bible and prayer.

I have not overcome this drama, but I will say my sons know the truth and stand on the Word as I do. We hold fast together and we hang on. We endure each storm and I have realized as much as it is painful, we are taught something through each trial.

God is—yesterday, today, and tomorrow, regardless of circumstance. I may not be loved as I had always dreamed of from an earthly husband, but the Lord can fill me. And my sons can overcome as the Lord leads them.

So, this is what makes each storm bearable: I know God is love, and with that love comes redemption and hope.

Debbie knows that even though she can't see through the storm to the other side, God is still there, calming the wind and waves and guiding her family to a place of redemption and renewed hope. Her hope in the midst of the storm is not in its outcome, but in the One who overcomes. She too has found her center in Christ.

Calming the Storm

Psalm 107 speaks of God's goodness to His people when they were wandering in the desert wastelands while hungry and thirsty, sitting in darkness and the deepest gloom, prisoners suffering in iron chains because of their rebellion, and sailing out on the stormy sea in ships. Even when they were running from God or resistant to His love, He still delivered them. And God does the same for us today when we feel overwhelmed by our circumstances.

I am especially encouraged by verses 28 through 30, which I find applicable to any storm you and I might possibly encounter today. Look at what happened when the Lord's people cried to Him from the center of their storm:

> They cried out to the LORD in their trouble,
> and he brought them out of their distress.

He stilled the storm to a whisper;
the waves of the sea were hushed.
They were glad when it grew calm;
and he guided them to their desired haven.

Living It Out

So in light of your drama—be it unexpected circumstances, unkind talk, unwarranted pain, or unwanted trials—what are you believing about God that isn't true? That He's not a refuge? That He doesn't care? That He isn't capable of caring for you and getting you through this? Capture those thoughts, and then correct your thinking by recounting who God really is. You'll find He is bigger than anything that concerns you and all that threatens to overwhelm you.

God is your center. He is your protector. He is your hiding place (Psalm 32:7). Now hide away in Him!

A Point to Process

We can still the drama in our lives when we find Christ as our center, not the one who helps us solve it all, but the One who helps us sort it through and brings us back to this one thing: God is a God of order.

A Truth to Consider

When you pass through the waters, I will be with you; and when you pass through the rivers, they will not sweep over you. When you walk through the fire, you will not be burned; the flames will not set you ablaze.
ISAIAH 43:2

A Focus for the Week

Capture your thoughts this week and correct your thinking by asking yourself, "What am I believing about God that isn't true?" each time you are disappointed, disillusioned, or depressed.

A Prayer from the Heart

Lord God, You are the Only One who can still the storm that threatens to overwhelm me. When I remember that You are in control and at the center of my circumstances as well as my being, I can get through anything. Thank You for Your promise that You will never leave me nor forsake me (Hebrews 13:5), especially when I become overwhelmed. Help me to trust You to stay at the helm, Lord Jesus, and lead me to Your desired haven.

Chapter 7

Scene Change— No Longer Overextended

Allowing Yourself an Intermission

*In our Lord's life there was none of the pressure and the
rushing of tremendous activity that we regard so highly
today, and a disciple is to be like His Master.*
OSWALD CHAMBERS

*Because so many people were coming and going that they did
not even have a chance to eat, he said to them, "Come with
me by yourselves to a quiet place and get some rest."*
MARK 6:31

Cyndie was the epitome of an overextended woman.
The oldest of several children and a mom of three grown
children, Cyndie many times felt responsible for caring for her
younger siblings (in addition to her own family), her coworkers,
and just about everyone else who relied on her for help. Because
she was kindhearted and struggled with the ability to say no, her

life became permeated with drama—until God intervened and got her attention through what I call a "forced intermission."

I asked Cyndie to share with you her journey from a stressed-out, overextended woman to one who is now drama free:

> A couple of months ago I realized that I was very unhappy with where I was in life, specifically with my job. It wasn't that I hated the job; I didn't. But there seemed to be an increased sense of discord among my coworkers, including myself, and it made me feel very unhappy.
>
> I worked with 20 women, which was often challenging because women possess the "drama" gene. On any given day one or more of us was moody, stressed, PMSing, had a sick child or husband or parent, was brokenhearted, had the car break down, was financially broke, or was feeling she had nothing else to give. Added to that were the responsibilities of the job, and it amounted to a recipe for a lot of drama!
>
> I was letting the hearsay of others poison my opinion of the job I was doing, and with each new day, I became more and more self-conscious and vulnerable to any comment or action that felt like proof of my incompetence. I'm convinced that the enemy will hit us at our weakest point, and for me that would be my feelings of self-worth.
>
> I learned at a very early age to be a "fixer." I discovered that by being the person everyone could depend on to make their situation better I would feel validated, important, and necessary to others. I was like a beacon, a flashing light calling everyone and anyone to run to me to help repair the broken

parts of their lives. Aren't we taught that we serve God first, others second, and ourselves last? I wish I had understood that in order to be that beacon of light to others, I had to tend to the light in *my* life first. After all, it's not my place to fix anybody; that job belongs to the Lord.

For too long I thought I was serving God by being there for others, but what I have discovered is that nothing could have been further from the truth. I thought that I was putting myself last, but the reality is that I was putting myself first, others second, and God last. I wasn't taking the time to get to know the Lord, to sit at the feet of Jesus and learn the sound of His voice. My prayer life was used for the times I was in need and desperate. (How quickly we forget to pray and study the Bible when things are going well.)

For more than a year I had been neglecting my health, not working out, and not taking time for some fun. I hadn't ridden my bike in two years! This past spring, I came down with a severe urinary tract infection and it put me in bed for three days. I was unable to even stand up without help. I'd never been so weak. My sweet husband stayed home from work and took care of me and suggested that I needed to be taking better care of myself, which might mean I should consider leaving my job. He, of course, was very aware of the toll all the drama at work was taking on me emotionally and physically. I agreed to consider his suggestion.

Lying there in my bed, I had plenty of time to spend with the Lord. I began praying and searching the Scriptures, listening for His voice to help me make a decision about my future. I realized that for quite a while God had been trying to get my attention, prompting me to make the very changes I was faced with while lying in that bed. I could see so many situations where He had been clearly guiding me, but I had chosen to ignore those. I didn't do it intentionally; I just thought those were my own self-ish thoughts of wanting to give up working. (That is why it's so important not to neglect your time spent in the Word, because that is how we learn to recognize the voice of the Lord.)

I also recognized that my need to leave my job was about more than just what was happening at work. My health had been declining, and on top of that, I had to prepare for a move since my husband was planning to retire the next year.

On the third day of being bedridden, I was asking God, specifically, if I needed to quit my job. I was wishing God would just send me a text message telling me what to do. If only! Before I went to sleep that night I made the decision to quit. I just decided to trust that if that wasn't the path to follow, God would make it clear. When I awoke the next morning, after one of the best night's sleep I've had in years (I struggle with insomnia), I had complete peace about my decision. I felt as though a huge weight had been lifted from my shoulders.

Cyndie was surprised to find out that many of her coworkers were sad to hear she was leaving. "Some were pretty emotional, and a few told me that they would miss my kindness and encouragement," she said. She discovered that she had impacted their lives in a positive way. That felt good to Cyndie to know she had made a difference there. Still, she knew she had made the right decision to move on…out of the drama and forward into another adventure in life.

We Really Can Change

Because Cyndie was able to successfully navigate that situation with God's help, she gained confidence that she really could control how she responds to her circumstances. And whether or not they are emotionally overwhelming is up to her. She also realized how quickly she could neglect taking care of herself when she became emotionally or physically overwhelmed.

Now Cyndie prioritizes God first in her life, and it results in her having the tools to balance the stress and drama that comes her way. And she can help others—specifically the young moms she mentors in her church—now that God has transformed her from a panicked woman to a peaceful one.

I believe the growth in Cyndie's relationship with Christ and her love for His Word prepared her to handle what came next.

Shortly after Cyndie quit her job, her husband was in the hospital for severe dehydration, and at the same time, her brother was diagnosed with lymphoma. Cyndie sent out a prayer request to her friends and family, and I noticed in it the absence of "Stressed-Out Cyndie" and the presence of "Spirit-Controlled Cyndie." She displayed grace under pressure and a peace in circumstances that ordinarily would've panicked her.

I commented to her about how the old Cyndie would have reacted and how the new Cyndie appeared to be taking all these dramatic events in stride. This was her response:

It has been a very challenging couple of weeks! However, I think God had been preparing me for something ahead. Even though there is a lot going on right now, I feel quite at peace, not fearful at all. Of course there is some stress, but I think it comes from the people and situations happening around me, not from within. I finally understand that I can just rest in Jesus and let Him do whatever needs to be done in the lives of others. I'm not God, thankfully! Of course I'm not emotionless; I care deeply about the people I love, but I'm choosing to let God be my Father to comfort me and assure me that He is in complete control. But believe me, all it takes is a minute or two of losing that focus and I'm slipping into "hand-wringing mode"!

Did you catch the key to Cyndie's peace? "I finally understand that I can just rest in Jesus and let Him do whatever needs to be done in the lives of others. I'm not God!"

Therein lies our drama, girlfriend. We at times insist on being the one to do whatever needs to be done in the lives of others, and that is God's job, not ours.

Stay Out of It

We often believe that simply because something happens in our sphere of influence, we are supposed to step in and fix it. Then there's drama because we feel overwhelmed at all we believe we have to do. But just because we are made *aware* of a situation doesn't mean God is *assigning* it to us. And just because someone asks for our help doesn't mean God is asking for it. When we discover someone is in need, we should stop, seek God's guidance, and then stay out of it if God doesn't give us the go-ahead.

Just to make sure you—and I—got that, I'm going to repeat that process:

- Stop.
- Seek God's guidance.
- Stay out of it if you don't get clear indication to step into it.

That last point is important because oftentimes God wants to do a special work in another person's life, and we unknowingly interfere.

Just because we are made *aware* of a situation doesn't mean God is *assigning* it to us.

Now, I'm not talking about refusing to help someone when it's within your means to do so. I'm talking about the God complex we tend to get, as women, when we believe we must rush in, ease the pain, and find a solution for someone when perhaps God led that person to a point of helplessness so she would find a saving knowledge or deeper reliance on Him.

The famous preacher Oswald Chambers wrote:

> If you become a necessity to someone else's life, you are out of God's will…When you see a person who is close to grasping the claims of Jesus Christ, you know that your influence has been used in the right direction. And when you begin to see that person in the middle of a difficult and painful struggle, don't try to prevent it, but pray that his difficulty will grow even ten times stronger, until no power on earth or in hell could hold him away from Jesus Christ. Over and over again, we try to be amateur providences in someone's life. We are indeed amateurs, coming in

and actually preventing God's will and saying "This person should not have to experience this difficulty." Instead of being friends with (Christ), our sympathy gets in the way.[1]

Don't be one who interferes with God's work in another's life because you rushed in to help without seeking God's direction and permission first.

Following Jesus' Example

Taking an intermission (although involuntary) was necessary for Cyndie to reevaluate her health, reprioritize her life, and recharge—so she could not only focus on the tasks God had for her, but listen in the first place to what it was He wanted her to focus on. When I wrote my book *When Women Long for Rest*, I gave several examples of how God will force rest upon us if we don't take it ourselves. He may allow an injury, a prolonged sickness, a broken leg (or two), a crashed computer, a lost cell phone, a delayed flight, or any number of other scenarios to get us to slow down, spend time with Him, and hear what He wants to say to us. He's not going to give us direction for our lives if we're running in circles and not listening.

God speaks to us in the stillness.
And Satan screams at us in our busyness.

It occurred to me recently that God speaks to us in the stillness. And Satan screams at us in our busyness. When I remain still, I can hear His quiet whisper. When I'm running harried, I only hear confusion and experience chaos.

Jesus modeled to us how to slip away from time to time so we don't find ourselves overextended and full of potential drama. In Mark 6 we read that "because so many people were coming and going that they did not even have a chance to eat, [Jesus] said to them, 'Come with me by yourselves to a quiet place and get some rest.' So they went away by themselves in a boat to a solitary place" (verses 31-32). In Mark 1 we read, "Very early in the morning, while it was still dark, Jesus got up, left the house and went off to a solitary place, where he prayed. Simon and his companions went to look for him, and when they found him, they exclaimed: 'Everyone is looking for you!'" (verses 35-37).

Jesus was quite the popular guy. Everyone wanted to be around Him, and when He went off by Himself, everyone was *looking* for Him. I find Jesus' response to the disciples' complaint very interesting:

> Jesus replied, "Let us go somewhere else—to the nearby villages—so I can preach there also. That is why I have come" (verse 38).

When Jesus heard that people were looking for Him, He didn't go back to meet their every need. He actually went *somewhere else*. "That is why I have come," He told His followers. He didn't come to enable, entertain, or even educate people. He certainly didn't come to eliminate future needs. He came to do His Father's will—no more, no less. So when the Father prompted Him to move on to another location (Jesus apparently got that instruction earlier in the morning when He rose early and prayed), He moved on.

Jesus constantly communed with His Father. I believe that's why He didn't do all that was humanly expected of Him. I mean, think about it. Just because there was a need didn't mean Jesus met it. Jesus clearly didn't:

- feed *all* the people who were hungry,
- heal *all* the sick and diseased,
- respond to *every* request that was made of Him, or
- take Israel out of Roman oppression (that wasn't His mission).

Instead, He did only what God had led Him to do. Because Jesus was clear on God's instructions in His life, He was able to say this to His Father before He went to the cross: "I have glorified You on the earth. I have *finished the work which You have given Me to do*" (John 17:4 NKJV).

Jesus knew exactly what He was supposed to do during His short time on this earth because He took time to be in close communion with His Father. As a result, He managed His time well too. Because He was so familiar with His mission, He was able to focus on God's specific will and not waste time on the demands and expectations of everyone else.

Oh, to be so in tune with God and His instructions for our lives that we are able to one day say to our heavenly Father the same thing Jesus did: "I have finished the work which You have given Me to do." And yet if we are continually overextended, with every block of time in our schedule booked, we will not be available for the work God brings our way. And we will not be able to tell God that we've finished the work He gave us. We will instead have to say something like, "Sorry, God. I was so busy doing all the things *everybody else* asked me to do that I failed to see the few important things *You* really wanted me to do."

Finding Your Focus

In order to finish the work God has given us, we first have to discover what it is. Then we need to say no to the less important things that compete with our time and devotion to Him.

In my book *When a Woman Discovers Her Dream*, as I share how women can discover what it is God calls them to do, I also lay out guidelines for discerning God's calling on our lives. One of those steps is for us to take our opportunities and possible involvement through the grid of three discerning questions:

1. **Is this something someone else can just as easily do?** If so, God is not specifically calling *you* to the task. Often God's will for you involves something that *only you* can do because of your background, your abilities, your relationships, and your equipping by God's Holy Spirit.

2. **Is this something I have a strong heart's desire to do?** God will not call us to do something we absolutely don't want to do. (Now He *will* call us to do something we don't feel capable of doing—He has a track record throughout Scripture of doing that because He wants to be the One to enable us to do it. But generally, He will call us to something He has convicted our hearts deeply about.)

3. **Is this something I feel God nudging me to do?** When God assigns us a task He will often confirm it over and over again so we not only get the hint but feel the push. If you can forget about a need without incident, then pondering whether to meet it was your idea. But if you don't have peace about it until you do it, then it was God's idea.

When you take these questions to the Lord and say, "God, please confirm to me if I am the one to do this" and then wait for His answer, you can be more certain that you are called to a specific task or ministry, and you can have greater assurance that God is going before you into it.

Take an Intermission

It's easy to talk about how much we need to rest. But until we actually do it, it's just talk. Here is the tried-and-true process I've had to practice in my own life, and not just once. Every time I start to feel overextended, I need to come back to these five steps to keep myself rested and available to God to accomplish what He wants for me specifically.

Realize God Wants You to Rest, Not Stress

When I wrote my book *When Women Long for Rest*, I learned that God would rather have us spend time *with* Him than do a bunch of things *for* Him. Our work for Him can be done out of a sense of obligation or our own efforts and strength. But our time with Him—listening to His quiet whispers on our hearts— is something that can only happen when we are intent on growing in our relationship with Him. God realizes that when we are too busy, we will get run down and won't be on our best game. We will make decisions that aren't the best, carry out actions that aren't the best, and begin to live a life that is bent on our preferences, not God's.

....

God would rather have us spend time *with* Him
than do a bunch of things *for* Him.

....

But when we spend time sitting at His feet, we will be able to hear what He wants to say to us, then get up and serve Him. When we worship Him through rest, we will eventually get up and work for Him. When we love Him, our labor will flow out of that love relationship. He is a God of rest, not a God of stress. So get rid of the guilt that you aren't *doing* enough for God.

Refuel Your Body Through a Healthier Lifestyle

My friend Gayla—who ministers at Word of Life Christian Center in Lone Tree, Colorado, alongside her husband—has seen many women divert drama in their lives by simply taking better care of themselves. "When women eat right and exercise regularly, they do better and cope easier with stress," she said. "Having a disciplined life of health, along with spiritual disciplines, helps a woman cope so much better when the drama of life hits."

Gayla said the key to being drama free in her own life is recognizing the need to take an intermission.

"Now that I'm 60, I've learned a few things about what a woman—including myself—can do to diffuse the drama in her life: eat healthy, exercise regularly, be disciplined in church attendance, read the Bible every day, pray about everything, listen to praise and worship music often, stop feeling guilty, and take more breaks."

Release the Things You Cannot Do

You know your limits. When you wake up in the morning and think *I can't do this one more time*, that's often your body and mind telling you to slow down, take a break, and cross something off your schedule.[2] Gayla has also learned the art of delegation and allowing others to share the load. "It's hard enough taking care of a staff of 50 people and 125 leaders over different areas, but then when we deal with hundreds of people and their problems and crises, it can really set anxiety into motion," Gayla said. "I am so thankful for the way God sends the right people to help share the load. He has taught me how to say no and how to release projects to others and how to take breaks and not feel guilty because He is a God of rest too."

Rely on God to Care for What You Can't

Donna, whose story is in chapter 2, learned of her mother's sudden death in a car accident and felt the pull to leave her business to travel and be with her extended family and help make final arrangements. Her mind was saying, *It's April, you can't leave …you have to be here for your spring promotions and to keep things running smoothly.* But God was saying, *Trust Me. Go do what you need to do.*

Donna left her center in the hands of capable women and substitute instructors to teach her classes. When she returned a month later, she found out her center had had the highest-grossing April on record! Then when she stepped away from her center a second time, this time for two months after receiving a breast cancer diagnosis, the center experienced its best two months ever financially. God was affirming to her, again, the principle that He can take care of more while we rest than we can while we work!

Resist the Urge to Step Back In

Often when we release something, we feel better about it if we think letting go is just temporary. I can't tell you how many Christian celebrities I've known who have had schedules that have been so stressful that they've experienced heart attacks or other stress-related health problems. As a result, they had no choice but to release many of their responsibilities. But as soon as they were healthy again, they got right back into the rat race, full speed ahead. Proverbs 26:11 says, "As a dog returns to its vomit, so fools repeat their folly." I know, that's pretty gross. It's pretty dramatic too. But that's what it's like when we go back and make the same mistake again … it's like returning to smelly puke. Don't do it. Stay in the slow lane, where you can live more simply and hear God's voice more clearly. You'll be glad you did.

Give Yourself a Break

Oswald Chambers said, "It is the innermost, personal arena that reveals the power of a person's life." What is going on in your personal arena? Is it a circus? A loud dance party? A silent dungeon? Or is it a peaceful sanctuary where you commune with God? Chambers again: "In our Lord's life there was none of the pressure and the rushing of tremendous activity that we regard so highly today, and a disciple is to be like His master. The central point of the Kingdom of Jesus Christ is a personal relationship with Him, not public usefulness to others."[3]

Are you ready to give yourself a break? Are you ready to move past the dramatic role of Superwoman, in which you feel you have to take care of every need around you? That is drama. And it's not what God expects of you. Instead of being Superwoman, depend on your Super God to do what you cannot, and listen to His command to rest.

A Point to Process

Just because something happens in your sphere of influence doesn't mean God is assigning you to run to the rescue and fix it. Much drama can be avoided when you get in the habit of running your schedule past God and asking Him what needs to go.

A Truth to Consider

Come to me, all of you who are weary and carry heavy burdens, and I will give you rest. Take my yoke upon you. Let me teach you, because I am humble and gentle at heart, and you will find rest for your souls. For my yoke is easy to bear, and the burden I give you is light.
MATTHEW 11:28-30 NLT

A Focus for the Week

Schedule an intermission into your week. This could be a one-hour walk in the park, an afternoon visit to a spa, or some time set aside to read a book, commune with God, and enjoy the quiet. Write here what you plan to do:

My Intermission

Date: _____

Time: _____

Place: _____

What to Bring: _____

Preparation (if any): _____

A Prayer from the Heart

Lord, You would rather have me spend time with You than do a bunch of things for You. Help me to see each day as a gift from You and live it wisely by following Your priorities so I don't overextend my schedule. My wig-outs and freak-outs often result from packing too much into my week without consulting with You first. Remind me, daily, that I was created to love You and enjoy You forever, and when I start to feel overextended, it's time to take an intermission and let You breathe rest back into my life.

Chapter 8

Scene Change– No Longer Self-Absorbed

Becoming Sensitive to the Plight of Others

In the natural life our ambitions are our own, but in the Christian life, we have no goals of our own.
OSWALD CHAMBERS

Do nothing from selfishness or empty conceit,
but with humility of mind regard one another as
more important than yourselves; do not merely
look out for your own personal interests, but also
for the interests of others.
PHILIPPIANS 2:3-4 NASB

*A*lena recalls with regret the day she was a drama queen.
I have found myself, more than a few times, crying as I reflect on memories involving drama in my life. I'm a pretty peaceful, even-keeled girl, but there

have been a few times in my life I have been anything but. As the saying goes, "Go big or go home." That's about the sum of it, although embarrassing.

Alena told me about the day she went to the voting polls several years ago. She'd had a rough day, to say the least. So when a volunteer at the polling place handed her her voter's registration card and repeatedly made unprofessional comments, implying she knew how Alena would vote, Alena came unglued. She made a full-fledged scene, shouting at the woman repeatedly. Aware of her shocking behavior but still enraged, she ran out of the room, screaming, shaking, and completely out of control.

I suppose every person in the room thought to themselves, *What is her problem? What a drama queen!* You and I might've thought the same thing. But you'd have to know the backstory to know why Alena reacted the way she did. You'd have to know what was really going on to determine who was the self-absorbed person at the polls that day.

Here is the whole story of that dreaded, embarrassing day in Alena's own words—and what we can learn from it:

> It was election day of 2000. Things had been heating up in the political world but my mind was far from politics. My days revolved around The Cancer Center of Pittsburgh. It was day 12 of my husband's hospital stay and his second course of chemotherapy.
>
> I had gone home for the night to be with our four children. They knew things were not good concerning their dad, but I didn't want them to worry too much, so I held a lot inside, emotionally. As I got out of the van and walked into the house, I found myself

covered with hugs, kisses, and questions about how their dad was doing that day.

I got them dinner, helped them get their homework done, and then answered the door. It was my friend, Jennifer. She would stop by after work to check on us and to see if I wanted to go out for a quick bite to eat. This time she asked if Rick and I were going to vote.

I told her we were, but he was in no condition to go and I didn't feel like it because it had been a long day.

"Come on. Let's go vote," Jennifer said. "I'll drive."

Jennifer drove me over to the fire hall, where I could cast my ballot. She waited in the car while I went inside with my voter's registration card in hand. An older woman was greeting people as they came in. She smiled at me and took my card. I smiled back. Staring at my card, her smile suddenly changed to a smirk.

"Ahhh, I see."

Handing it back, she said in a sarcastic voice, "Well, I hope you have social security when you retire."

Puzzled, I looked at her and said, "Excuse me?"

Swaying her hips back and forth and looking rather smug, she repeated: "I hope you have social security when you retire."

It took me a moment to figure out what she was getting at. Glancing around, I saw some other older people sitting there staring at me. I was very uncomfortable, but I smiled. She continued with her digs, and with all the calmness I could muster up I said, "Ma'am, please stop. You have no idea what you are talking about."

Without any hesitation, she said, "You better hope you have social security when you and your husband get old."

I felt everything inside of me rise to the surface like a pressure cooker. I felt my face turn red and my body becoming hot all over. I looked at her and, through clenched teeth and low voice, I said, "You need to shut up. You have no idea what you are talking about."

With her still-smug expression and a mouth dripping with sarcasm, she said, "Well, you don't have to be like that."

I felt it. Something snapped. A tidal wave of tears began running down my face as I screamed at her.

"You shut up, lady. You don't know what you are talking about. My husband is in the hospital right this very moment dying. JUST SHUT UP! SHUT UP!"

The woman stood there staring at me with a startled look on her face. She tried to tell me to stop, but I kept screaming at her. I turned to go out the door and she yelled, "You can't go out there like that." Stopping, I turned around and said, "Oh yeah? Watch me! You can't tell me what to do!"

Pushing the door open, I walked back to my friend's car. Jennifer, looking bewildered, reached over to unlock the door. The woman opened the door and yelled for me to come back inside and not to leave that way. I screamed at her again to leave me alone.

I opened the car door to get in and looked back toward the firehouse. There stood some firemen who had come out to see what all the commotion was.

Jennifer looked at me in disbelief and asked, "What is going on?"

I told her what had happened with the woman.

"You go back in there and vote. I'll go with you. If she says anything to you, keep walking, and I'll take care of her."

Slamming the door as I got out, I said, "This one is for Rick."

Upon entering the firehouse hall, the woman started to address me. Without looking at her, I cut her off mid-sentence by holding my hand up in front of her face. With tears streaming and my head held high, I walked past her and into the hall where the voting booths were. To add more misery to my embarrassment, there stood George, whom the kids in my neighborhood called "The Neighborhood Grouch." *Great, this is all I need,* I thought to myself. *He'll tell the whole neighborhood that the pastor's wife just went insane.*

Through my tears, I saw him standing in the middle of the room with his arms wide open. With uncontrollable sobs, I walked quickly to his embrace.

"There, there," he said. "It will be all right. I'm so sorry. So, so sorry."

With my head buried in his soft flannel shirt, I

cried, "I don't know what to do. What do I have to do?"

He walked me over to the table to sign in, and then directed me to the voting booth. I stepped inside, eyes blurred with tears and my mind filled with unsteady emotions, which made it impossible for me to figure out how to close the curtain. George stepped in and pulled the lever.

With each click that I made while casting votes, I kept thinking about Rick. He would have been there, proudly casting his votes. With each thought, more tears came. By this point, I ceased caring if people heard me crying. What difference did it make? They had already heard me screaming.

When I finished voting, I turned, pulled back the curtain…and there stood George. He hugged me, once again telling me it would be all right, and we said our good-byes. Jennifer was by the door waiting for me. She put her arm around me as we walked past the woman at the door. She was trying to say something to me but I didn't hear her. I let Jennifer handle it this time.

Once in the car, I started laughing and I couldn't stop. Then I started to cry again. Jennifer kept questioning me about the incident. She said she could hear me screaming all the way out to the parking lot. She wasn't sure what had happened inside.

As we drove down the highway, I told her what had taken place. We exited off the freeway and right at that moment, I let out an ear-piercing scream. It caused Jennifer to jump and almost drive us off the road. Between being scared and laughing, she yelled, "Alena! Let me know the next time you do that. I'll put the windows down first. You *scared* me!"

I refer to that night as the night I went insane. Jennifer says that is the night I broke from insanity.

Who Is to Blame?

Alena had been hit with something so overwhelming she hardly knew how to process it, let alone deal with the catty remarks of a stranger. Her husband had been diagnosed with lymphoma two weeks earlier. He ended up dying just two weeks after that incident at the polls. So who was the cause of the drama at the polls that day?

Was it Alena because she erupted over an unsolicited comment that cut deep and triggered her anger, frustration, and fear that her husband was dying? Or was it the woman with the catty comment, who was thinking only of her political agenda and not how painful an ill-timed remark could be? How could that woman have possibly known her reference to Alena's husband getting old would trigger an emotional meltdown from Alena as she was already dealing with the certainty of Rick dying young?

How often you and I might think of our own agenda and not realize how very painful an ill-timed remark could be.

Alena is an example of how the people around us can be hurting, and we often have *no* idea what they're facing. Until they blow up in a dramatic scene. Until they fall apart at a comment we make about them or their child. Until they erupt in anger when things go wrong at the store checkout line. Until we read about them in the paper the next morning because they drove their car over a bridge.

An inability to see beyond ourselves can make you and me the ultimate drama queen. It can make us the catalyst for a dramatic eruption in someone else. How can we possibly know if something we say might trigger an assault of repressed emotions from someone who is struggling with some pain? We can't. But if we come outside ourselves long enough to focus on others around us and apply the Bible's advice about restraining our words, it will help us not only dial down the drama in our own lives, but possibly prevent it from erupting in others' lives as well.

Restraining Our Words

Over time, I've come to realize that those who are older tend to know the secret to living drama free. They tend to listen more than they speak. Now there's always the exception—maybe you've got a grouchy relative who doesn't restrain his words at all. Or maybe you have an older woman in your neighborhood who is quite the gossip. But for the most part, I've found that maturity exists in those who have lived long enough to know when they should restrain their words.

Drama tends to happen when we feel we have something to "contribute" to a situation whether we're invited to or not. I knew someone who called this "therapy."

"For years I kept silent about whatever bothered me. No more! I now say what I feel, no matter what anyone else thinks," she said with a proud tone. That same woman has hurt many people I love through her proud new habit of "saying whatever I feel" instead of using discernment in the moment and finding a healthier way to respond.

Consider what the Bible says about the indiscreet habit of "saying whatever I feel" or feeling the need to speak into everything:

- "Those who *guard their lips* preserve their lives,
  but those who speak rashly will come to ruin"
  (Proverbs 13:3).

- "The one who has knowledge *uses words with restraint,*
  and whoever has understanding is even-tempered"
  (Proverbs 17:27).

- "Even fools are thought wise if they *keep silent,*
  and *discerning if they hold their tongues*"
  (Proverbs 17:28).

- "Those who *guard their mouths and their tongues*
  keep themselves from calamity"
  (Proverbs 21:23).

....

When we guard our mouths and restrain our words,
we won't accidentally stoke a fire that is
smoldering and ready to blaze.

....

When we guard our mouths and thereby restrain our words,
we won't accidentally stoke a fire that is smoldering and ready
to blaze. We won't be tripping the switch that sets off the time
bomb. We won't inadvertently worsen the hurt a person is struggling with.

Avoiding the Ticking Bomb

Some women are more emotional than others. And that
means they could be about to lose it at any moment over their circumstances, their pain, their stress, or their slight inconvenience.
My friend Brenda offered some insight on how others' dramatic
outbursts can show us something about how they are hurting.

Often it's in those drama moments that we can learn more or gain understanding about what hurts or hang-ups others may have. If we really desire to be others-focused and have a genuine concern for their well-being, these moments allow us insight on how to intercede in prayer for others. We must be careful, though, to keep the intercession to biblical principles, Christ-centered counsel, and so on. This is not to say we should seek to *cause* drama to learn these things about others, but be a good observer and then use the opportunity to glorify God rather than entertain the devil.

Steps to Being Selfless

These tips will help you—and me—be more others-focused so we don't cause drama for someone else.

Consider the Other Person Above Yourself

Doing this does not come naturally. It is human nature to think of ourselves. But in a saving relationship with Christ, we have a new nature, one that puts others first. The Bible instructs us to "do nothing from selfishness or empty conceit, but with humility of mind regard one another as more important than yourselves" (Philippians 2:3 NASB).

Consider Your Words Carefully

In Ephesians 4:29, we are exhorted to "not let any unwholesome talk come out of your mouths, but only what is helpful for building others up according to their needs, that it may benefit those who listen." This means repressing the urge to give someone a "piece of your mind" when you've been inconvenienced or you (or your child or friend) has been treated unfairly. Your complaint might be the last one that person can take before having a meltdown.

Choose to be a Listener

We are told in James 1:19 to be "quick to listen, slow to speak and slow to become angry." Yet how natural it is for us to react first, then calm down and rethink the situation later. When we focus on listening rather than responding, we can learn so much more about others and be ready to help them more in the long run.

My friend Donna (whose series of unfortunate events you read about in chapter 2) says she is much more aware of people around her and what they might be going through now that she's experienced cancer and the sudden death of both of her parents. She knows what it's like to stand in the grocery store with the world swirling around her and wonder if a year from that moment she'll still be buying food for her family. She knows what it's like to be going through a crisis that has changed her world when everyone else is oblivious to what's happening. Her difficult season of life has made her more sensitive to what other people may be going through. That, my friend, is the key to not being self-absorbed.

"Comfort In, Dump Out"

My friend Allison shared with me an article on the "Ring Theory of Kvetching (Incessant Complaining)." It's basically a concept about how to support and respond to someone who needs comfort, without giving advice or creating additional emotional burdens. Married to a cancer survivor, Allison learned what we have a right to speak into and when we shouldn't say anything at all.

We all want to say to a person with cancer, "I don't think I can handle losing you. This is hard on me," but those words aren't appropriate for someone dealing with far more than you are. The patient is dealing with the possibility of losing *her own* life and shouldn't have to shoulder your burden on top of hers.

The concept behind the "Ring Theory of Kvetching," according to Susan Silk and Barry Goldman, is to draw a circle. This is the center ring. In it, put the name of the person at the center of the current trauma. In the case of Donna's cancer, that would be Donna. Then draw a larger circle around the first one. In that ring put the name of the person next closest to the trauma. In Donna's case, that would be her husband, Greg. Repeat the process as many times as you need to. In each larger ring put the next closest people. Parents and children before more distant relatives. Intimate friends in smaller rings, less intimate friends in larger ones. That is the Kvetching Order.

Silk and Goldman explain the rules:

> The person in the center ring can say anything she wants to anyone, anywhere. She can kvetch and complain and whine and moan and curse the heavens and say, "Life is unfair" and "Why me?" That's the one payoff for being in the center ring.
>
> Everyone else can say those things too, but only to people in larger rings.
>
> When you are talking to a person in a ring smaller than yours, someone closer to the center of the crisis, the goal is to help. Listening is often more helpful than talking. But if you're going to open your mouth, ask yourself if what you are about to say is likely to provide comfort and support. If it isn't, don't say it. Don't, for example, give advice. People who are suffering from trauma don't need advice. They

need comfort and support. So say, "I'm sorry" or "This must really be hard for you" or "Can I bring you a pot roast?" Don't say, "You should hear what happened to me" or "Here's what I would do if I were you." And don't say, "This is really bringing me down."

If you want to scream or cry or complain, if you want to tell someone how shocked you are or how icky you feel, or whine about how it reminds you of all the terrible things that have happened to you lately, that's fine. It's a perfectly normal response. Just do it to someone in a bigger ring.

The whole idea of the Kvetching Order is "comfort in, dump out."[1]

What I like about that process is that it lets us know clearly when we can be self-absorbed and when we can't. And we have to be checking ourselves, constantly, to see if what we are about to say is appropriate to the person to whom we are saying it. Isn't that a practical way of practicing Ephesians 4:29, which instructs us to speak no unwholesome word, but only words good for building others up? I think so.

A Strategy When Someone Else Is Self-Absorbed

We've looked at what to do to keep someone *else* from erupting. But what if you are the Alena in the room and someone is provoking you or acting completely self-absorbed? What do you do if you read a Facebook post that ticks you off or someone says something to you and it's the last match to set off your fireworks show? Here are three steps that will help keep your emotions in check:

1. *Take a breather.* In the heat of the moment, take time to

step back, take a deep breath, and reevaluate. This will keep your emotions in check and keep you from flying off at someone. You've heard the expression "sleep on it" when you're faced with making a difficult decision. That's great advice when it comes to responding to an accusatory e-mail, an angry phone call, or a social media post that ruffled your feathers. Studies show that the brain actually processes situations more thoroughly while you sleep so that means you wake up with a fresh—and often less emotional—perspective. So, take a breather, get some perspective, and let the extra time cool the heat of your emotions.

2. *Take a personal inventory.* In every situation there is a lesson to be learned. And in every accusation there is a seed of truth. A drama-filled woman says "I must defend myself. I must clear my name. I must straighten this person out." But a mature woman lets God work in her heart by exposing to her any shred of truth in the accusation. It's easy for us to want to be loud and proud and prove our point in the heat of the moment. But when we step out of the battle and ask God to speak truth to our hearts, we are acknowledging that we make mistakes too, and we are willing to learn from the situation how to better respond next time. Doing this is humbling ourselves and letting God lift us up at the proper time (1 Peter 4:6).

3. *Take it to God.* I have found that when I am plagued by a situation that could cause drama, it is diffused when I take it to God and sit there with Him in it for a while. As I ask Him to help me see the situation more clearly, not only does He show me my part in it, but He also gives me wisdom to know how to respond next.

Sometimes a matter isn't worth pursuing further after we've set it at God's feet. Author Lysa TerKeurst says in her book *Unglued*, "When we are in the heat of a tangled mess, crazy emotions drag us down into a pit of hopelessness. The only way out of the pit is to make the choice to stop digging deeper and turn to God for a solution…"[2]

> Sometimes a matter isn't worth pursuing further after we've set it at God's feet.

When God Changes Us

When we are struggling, we may feel we have a right to be self-absorbed. We deserve the right to vent, explode, be dramatic. And yet Jesus went through the toughest time of anyone who walked this earth. He died an excruciating death at the hand of the brutal Romans on false charges by the Jewish religious elite, and He did it out of love for us and out of a desire to be obedient to His Father.

As He hung on the cross being mocked, He called out, "Father, forgive them, for they do not know what they are doing" (Luke 23:34). Jesus wasn't self-absorbed. Instead, He showed amazing love and forgiveness for those who wanted to see Him dead. That tells me that when we are suffering, we too can still think of others.

Barbara, whose story you read in chapter 6, e-mailed me a few days after her report of being overwhelmed by her cancer and her mother's dementia. Her e-mail showed me not only that she still had her center but that God was continuing to transform her into a woman who considered others above herself:

As I awoke this morning with a migraine and was

preparing to go to my mom's to get her up, she called. I was expecting her call to let me know she was awake but found out that, with resolve coming from her determination, she had gotten up, gotten to her computer, then to the couch, and was letting me know she was okay.

After arriving at my mom's place and getting her all set up with breakfast, newspapers, TV guide, remote, and phone, I told her I'd take a quick walk, shower, and be back in two hours.

I headed off and passed a man pushing a woman in a wheelchair. The woman had such empty eyes.

I didn't have that. How fortunate I was! That realization triggered tears as I expressed thanks out loud to God as I continued to walk.

I hadn't listened to my healing Scriptures for weeks, but I happened to turn them on my phone as I walked, reciting them aloud, realizing healing is so much deeper than relief from disease and having good health. God heals our perception, our trust, our expectations.

Cindi, when I was leaving to take my walk and my mom smiled up at me, I asked her how she did it. She said, "I just thought I had to do this for Barbara." I'm sobbing as I write you. I never begged God to strengthen her legs. I devolved into my self-centered sorrow of what I accepted as deterioration and felt I needed to beg God for strength and wisdom for me.

Shaking my head, I sobbed at that realization and continued to walk. I sobbed again when I told my husband later that day and shared it with my daughter when she called. As I put Mom in bed last night,

I said, "Let's pray that you're stronger tomorrow." I had never prayed, nor begged God, for restoration— for restored strength for her, for a delay in this process. And yet He gave it—restoration, strength, delay in the deterioration. The Spirit of God went before me and interceded what needed to be prayed. It was all about me and my weariness, my strength, my broken heart, and my need for wisdom, and yet He did this for me and her while reminding me that I should go deeper with Him in all aspects of my crying out to Him, to set aside the obvious (that which the world and the flesh presents as what's next) and to slow down, breathe, and ask myself, *What is it I need? For her legs to be strengthened!*

Barbara realized that even in a situation where it *is* all about us and our health and our sanity and our peace of mind, God's Spirit in us can give us a heart to intercede for others, to regard others as more important than ourselves. As we become more Spirit-filled, we will become more drama free.

Becoming like Christ

Christ's love for us was dramatically unselfish. In Philippians 2:5-8 (NLT), we see a description of Jesus' sacrifice on our behalf, and it serves as a model for us when we are tempted to be self-absorbed:

> You must have the same attitude
> that Christ Jesus had.
> Though he was God,
> he did not think of equality with God
> as something to cling to.
> Instead, he gave up his divine privileges;

he took the humble position of a slave
and was born as a human being.
When he appeared in human form
he humbled himself in obedience to God
and died a criminal's death on a cross.

Christ's love for us was dramatically unselfish.

You and I will never be asked to die a criminal's death on a cross. But we *are* asked to take on the humble task of serving and loving others, regardless of how we feel. Would you like to set aside concern for self no matter what you are experiencing? Then remember what Jesus' unselfish love did for you. That will help you model unselfish love—not drama—toward others.

A Point to Process

I can be drama free when I think of others above myself, whether I'm speaking, acting, or reacting.

A Truth to Consider

(Love) bears all things, believes all things,
hopes all things, endures all things. Love never fails.
1 CORINTHIANS 13:7-8 NASB

A Focus for the Week

Open your eyes to notice others around you. Ask, genuinely, how their day is going, and wait for an answer. Smile at others, and listen for what they are really saying when they express fear, frustration, anger, or annoyance.

A Prayer from the Heart

God, help me to show the kind of love toward others that Jesus showed, even when I'm inconvenienced, even when I'm frustrated, even when I'm hurting, and even when someone is being dramatically selfish toward me. Help me to remember Your selfless love and respond to others as You would respond to them.

Act III

Improving the Scene

Now that you have some scene changers and strategies in place, you can finally close the curtain on drama and start a new opening act—one in which you yield the spotlight to the Director of your story and impact others by how you live.

Chapter 9

Closing the Curtain

Putting an End to Drama

*We should battle through our moods, feelings, and emotions into
absolute devotion to the Lord Jesus. We must break out of our own
little world of experience into abandoned devotion to Him.*
OSWALD CHAMBERS

*When the storm has swept by, the wicked are gone,
but the righteous stand firm forever.*
PROVERBS 10:25

There comes a time when we have to say, "Enough!"
Enough of the heartache. Enough of this way of life.
Enough of the drama!

Rhonda remembers the day she said it to God. In her mind
she was telling Him, "I quit. I can't do this anymore." But in God's
plan it was just the beginning of His outpouring of blessings.

Rhonda Stoppe is a close friend of mine who writes, speaks,
and mentors women as a pastor's wife, mother, Bible teacher, and

author. But she had her share of drama in her young mommy years.[1]

In her book *Moms Raising Sons to be Men*, Rhonda tells the story of her son, Brandon, who had his first epileptic seizure at the age of six. What she hoped was a one-time occurrence turned out to be a condition that followed him through most of his childhood.

Rhonda wrote in her book:

> Daily I wrestled with my thoughts of fear and disappointment. *How had this become our life? All had been so normal—but in a moment, everything changed.* The hopes we'd had for our son's future were suddenly lost in a haze of doctor's visits, seizures, and medications.[2]

Then, after missing just one dose of medication, Brandon had another seizure—this time while Rhonda and her husband were ministering to a couple hundred teenagers from their church's youth group.

"I went upstairs because it just did me in," Rhonda told me. "I went up to my room, crying, and I said, *Lord, I quit. We're doing all this for You, pouring into all these kids downstairs, and You won't heal my kid? I'm done!*"

It was a raw, dramatic, bitter moment. And she felt justified in her feelings. Until God's Word pierced her heart: "In everything give thanks, for this is God's will for you in Christ Jesus" (1 Thessalonians 5:18 NASB).

"It was then that I surrendered and thanked God for it anyway," Rhonda said. "I remember saying, *God, my heart isn't on board. I will say 'thank You' with my lips, because that's what You tell me to do, but You'll have to change my heart.*"

And that's exactly what God did as He began to unfold *His* plan for Brandon's life.

As God started shaping Brandon in a different direction, Rhonda learned to trust His script for her son's life. Because Brandon was medicated, he didn't pursue sports, which was initially disappointing to his parents, who envisioned him as a star athlete. Brandon pursued music instead, and he became an accomplished musician who eventually ended up touring with several well-known Christian music artists.

As the Lord molded Brandon's love for music, it gradually began to dawn on Rhonda and her husband that God was preparing Brandon to accomplish *His* dreams for Brandon *His* way. Rhonda wrote:

> My vision had been the glory of the crowd cheering as Brandon passed the football, sunk a basket, or knocked one out of the park. God's plan was to fashion a musician who would glorify Him.
>
> My motive was to hear others praise the ability of *my* son. God's motive was, through Brandon, to lead many to praise *His* Son.
>
> I can say with absolute confidence and assurance that Brandon's seizure activity was God's way of preparing him for service to Him. Along the way, we learned to surrender our dreams for Brandon and replace them with God's plans for him.[3]

Today, Rhonda is concerned about her oldest daughter, Meredith, who has experienced several miscarriages and whose second child was born with physical disabilities. At the time of this writing, Meredith is pregnant again, and Rhonda has surrendered the situation to God once again.

"My concern over Meredith's pregnancy could be drama today," Rhonda said. "But knowing God loves her even more than I do, and knowing God knows all about what's ahead, I can rest in Him rather than worry, fear, or bring drama to the situation.

"I can't do drama. But I *can* do all things through Christ who strengthens me," Rhonda said, quoting Philippians 4:13.

When Rhonda said "Enough!" to the drama in her son's life so many years ago, she had no idea she was, by her surrender to God, closing the curtain on *her* drama and inviting God to intervene into her story—and her children's stories—for His glory.

Building on a Firm Foundation

In chapter 2 we learned that we can dial down the drama when we accept God's script for our lives. Rhonda had to accept God's script for her children's lives, too, in order to experience peace. It really comes down to acknowledging the fact that God is in control of our circumstances, and we are in control of our responses.

Throughout this book you've learned strategies for dealing with different kinds of drama. But closing the curtain on drama as a result of our small story, and becoming a part of God's greater story, comes down to three basic steps. Let's call them the ABCs to Diffusing Drama:

A—Acknowledge God is in control.

B—Build on a firm foundation.

C—Cultivate a heart of forgiveness.

In nearly every chapter, we've looked at how we can acknowledge that God is in control. Another way to say this is "accept

God's script for your life." Now let's look at what it means to build on a firm foundation.

Proverbs 10:25 tells us: "When the storm has swept by, the wicked are gone, but the righteous stand firm forever." When the storm of Brandon's seizure activity threatened to sweep Rhonda away, she stood firm. She didn't crumble under the pressure or get swept away in the drama, because she had built her life, years before, on a firm foundation. She had built her hopes, expectations, and very life on Christ, her rock.

Jesus told a parable to illustrate what it means to build on a firm foundation. He likened it to building a house on a rock, not sand:

> Therefore everyone who hears these words of mine and puts them into practice is like a wise man who built his house on the rock. The rain came down, the streams rose, and the winds blew and beat against that house; yet it did not fall, because it had its foundation on the rock. But everyone who hears these words of mine and does not put them into practice is like a foolish man who built his house on sand. The rain came down, the streams rose, and the winds blew and beat against that house, and it fell with a great crash (Matthew 7:24-27).

Are you one who stands firm when the storm sweeps by? You will if you have built your "house"—your expectations, hopes, dreams, and plans—on Christ the Rock and His Word. In contrast, when we build our expectations, hopes, dreams, and plans on sand (anything other than God), we will crumble as soon as someone disappoints us or circumstances overwhelm us. The sand shifts, but the Rock is steady. The sand blows away, but the

Rock stands firm. The sand washes away, but the Rock endures forever.

Rhonda wasn't born with that firm foundation. She was born on shaky ground, just like all of us. She had to start building on the Rock so she wouldn't repeat the cycle of dysfunctional drama that characterized most of the women in her family. "I grew up addicted to drama," Rhonda said. "Most of the women in my family were addicted to something—Valium, alcohol, prescription drugs. They self-medicated rather than dealing with the disappointments of life. God helped me to see that I could easily follow the same path unless I did things differently. So I chose to trust in the God who knows my story."

To build this solid foundation, Rhonda spent much of her time investing in the Word of God by memorizing Scripture and taking every thought captive to the obedience of Christ (remember that concept from chapter 6?). She constantly compared the world's advice with the Word's advice. The more she invested in God's Word, the stronger her foundation became.

And the result? Today, the storms of life don't sweep her away. Drama doesn't get the best of her. "Naturally I can be anxious about my kids, and my grandkids, and all that's happening with them," Rhonda said. "But the antidote to worry and stress and drama is that I can seek His kingdom first and His righteousness." There she goes again, quoting Scripture, this time Matthew 6:33.

"I can also decide that I'm not going to sit here and follow this path of destructive thinking in my mind. If I stop and say, 'I can't do a thing about any of this, but God can,' that reminds me to pray and leave it in His hands. If the effective, fervent prayer of a righteous person avails much (James 5:16), then I am diminishing the potential of my prayer life by entertaining unrighteous thoughts."

Rhonda admits that everyone has their weakness when it comes to drama. And hers is when someone attacks her family.

"As a pastor's wife, it's hardest when someone carelessly says stuff that is hurtful. In most cases I don't even think it's intentional, just thoughtless. Words that undermine the character of my husband hurt the worst because I know his heart. Even if you graciously smile and take whatever they say to you, you play it back in your mind later, you go over all the things you wish you had said in response. That's when we need to be forgiving so we can nip the drama in the bud.

....

When we forgive others quickly, it eliminates our opportunity to dwell on the drama.

....

Cultivating a heart of forgiveness is the third essential to being drama free. When we forgive others quickly, it eliminates our opportunity to dwell on the drama. It helps us, instead, to see others as God sees them and to love them as God does.

Exchanging Drama for Friendship

When I was in college, I attended my boyfriend's church. But it bothered me to see my boyfriend's ex-girlfriend, Shelley, who also attended that church with her family. Maybe it bothered me because I felt threatened by her. But she didn't seem to be bothered by my presence at all. Regardless, the fact that we were both there could have caused drama. And it had already started to in my mind as I found myself being critical of her and starting to have hateful thoughts.

So one Sunday I asked Shelley if we could get together and hang out sometime. I figured if I got to *know* her, I would probably like her, and there would be no reason for me to be jealous or critical of her any longer.

"Sure," she said. She gave me her phone number, and I called her that week. We decided to have lunch together, see a movie, and then go to the mall. While at lunch, I straight-out told her, "I'm tired of feeling jealous of you and Dennis, and I decided it would be much easier to become friends with you instead." She laughed and said, "At first I wondered why you wanted to get together, and my mom said, 'Maybe she just wants to be friends.' I'm glad I gave you a chance."

I'm glad I took the initiative to build a friendship with Shelley rather than resent her. She and I not only became friends, but we stayed friends after I broke up with Dennis. Getting to know someone can rid us of our assumptions and our critical nature, because often we don't know what we don't know. Exchanging potential drama for a friendship was a good exchange. I've done this repeatedly when I've met women whom I initially felt threatened around.

Terri learned this lesson as well when her daughter was in elementary school. I asked Terri to share her story in her own words:

> One day when I wasn't working, I decided to go to Megan's school and have lunch with her. The school had a special tradition: When parents came for lunch, they and their child could eat on the stage in the cafeteria, with tables set with nice tablecloths and flowers.
>
> When I arrived at my daughter's first-grade classroom, I noticed she was standing up at her desk! Megan was tall for her age, so you couldn't miss her. The teacher came to the door and explained that

Megan had fallen out of her chair, so she had to stand for the rest of the day!

My initial reaction was rage, but I stayed calm, and Megan and I got our lunches and sat on the stage to eat. I asked her about falling out of her chair and the punishment it entailed. She started crying and said she didn't mean to fall out on the floor. She said her back hurt from bending over to write her schoolwork and read. She was already a shy child, and the punishment was embarrassing for her.

I asked Megan if she wanted to go home with me. She bravely said she wanted to stay at school because she just wanted to get it over with and feared the teacher would be even angrier if she went home early. She asked if I would pray for her throughout the rest of the day (she had accepted Jesus as her Savior in kindergarten, so she already had a relationship with Christ). I silently prayed about what I should do as we finished our lunches. I knew I had to talk to the principal about this before I left.

I hate conflict and drama, so I felt sick in my stomach and my heart was pounding. I didn't want to create waves, but I knew the punishment didn't fit the "crime" for these poor little kids. I had to speak up—even if it meant I was going to create drama for our family at the school.

After Megan returned to class, I stopped in the office and asked to speak to the principal. I explained what had happened and said I didn't think it was fair. I pointed out that this only humiliated the children. The principal asked if I would speak to the teacher

first, which was the normal procedure for their
school. I told him I would, but I wanted this to stop
or I would speak to the school board about it. He told
me the certified school staff would consider what I
said, and he would get back with me.

I called my moms prayer group and asked them
to pray about all of this. I told them I wanted God
to use me in this situation for His glory—to bring
about a change. I wanted the teacher (who wasn't a
mom yet) to feel convicted and have a tender heart
for the children she had under her care.

I made an appointment to speak to the teacher
and explained to her exactly what I'd said to the
principal. I was kind but firm in our conversation. Megan's teacher told me she "had always done
it this way, and no one had ever complained." In
the end, she did not say if she would change her
procedure.

After another week of prayer, I called the principal, and he assured me the school would no longer
have children stand as punishment for falling out of
their chairs.

Later that school year, Megan's teacher asked if
any parents would volunteer to help in the classroom
during the day. My work hours had been shortened,
so I volunteered to help one afternoon a week. I was
very nervous because of our past drama. I prayed
the Lord would use me in the teacher's life to be an
example of what it is to be a Christian woman who
loves and fears the Lord. I knew being with her every
week was a God-ordained opportunity.

The hardest part at first was controlling the part of me that wanted to hold a grudge and be critical of her. But as I prayed for her and continued to work with her, it became easier to show her love through my attitudes and actions as each week went by.

Before the end of the school year, she asked our family to take care of her beloved dog while she and her husband were on vacation! She even invited my daughter and preschool-aged son and myself to go for a ride on her boat and have lunch one weekend.

Several years later, I learned that she became a mom and quit her teaching job to be a stay-at-home mommy.

I knew the Lord allowed all that to happen, and I felt so blessed to be able to pray for that woman every week during that school year. Praying faithfully led me to forgive her and changed my heart to love her with unconditional love. All these years later my daughter and I will often think of her and wonder how she is doing.

When my daughter wonders if she should intervene on uncomfortable, potentially drama-filled situations with my grandson at daycare, I remind her that she has to speak up for him, and that the Lord will direct her steps and guide her mouth. All she has to do is make sure she gives the situation to the Lord.

I am so glad that I obeyed God and left all the consequences with Him concerning that drama with Megan's first-grade teacher. God was glorified in the situation! And our family gained a friend. Drama that God allows is worth it when you walk with Jesus.

Is there someone in your life whom you have assumed might be drama simply because you don't know her or trust her? And is there a relationship in which you need to extend forgiveness in order to close the curtain on any potential or real drama? Consider exchanging that drama for a friendship, and see what God will do with it.

Now, if you are struggling with a much deeper offense and find forgiveness not only difficult but seemingly impossible at times, I understand. I've heard many stories from women who struggle daily with forgiving an offender. For a clearer understanding of what it means to forgive someone (it does *not* mean having to meet with that person face-to-face or resuming a relationship with them, nor does it mean waiting for them to admit they were wrong) see my article, "Should You Forgive Someone Who Isn't Sorry?"—which is available free on my website.[4]

A Strategy for Closing the Curtain

Throughout this book, I've shared strategies for diffusing drama in your life. Now I want to help you close the curtain on it. These four steps will constantly remind you that your response to others or your circumstances is the key to avoiding drama.

Consider the Source

People who hurt, hurt people. If someone gets hurt easily, complains at every turn, and has many relationship problems, she is most likely the problem. Simply put, if Amy has a problem with Susan, and Amy has a problem with Christy, and Amy has a problem with Gina, then Amy is most likely the problem. Likewise, if someone is mad and spews her words all over you, and you take the wound deeply, and then she gets over it and blows it off the next time you meet, that's a good indication she's the kind of person who treats everyone that way. It isn't personal. It probably isn't about you at all. So consider the source.

Consider God's Track Record

We've established by now that when we are hit with the unexpected or the disappointing, we can be all drama. But we can nip that drama in the bud when we stop fighting it or complaining about it and instead trust God with what He is doing to make us more like Christ. Look back at the providence of God and know that "He who began a good work in you will perfect it until the day of Christ Jesus" (Philippians 1:6 NASB). Then go to Scripture and look not at what certain people did, but at what *God* did. And what does that say about God's character? For example...

- God allowed Abraham and Sarah to be without a child for a long time, even after God promised them they would have one. But God also gave them a tremendous blessing in their old age.

- God allowed Moses to grow up in Egypt, but He also shaped him into the man who would lead His people out of oppression.

- God allowed Joseph to be sold into slavery, but God also allowed him to be elevated to the number-two ruler over all of Egypt.

....

God has an excellent track record of
honoring those who trust Him.

....

If God allows circumstances to come your way that you don't understand and certainly don't like, don't fret. He knows what

He's doing. And He has an excellent track record of honoring those who trust Him.

Consider the Seed

I mentioned this in chapter 8, but it's so valuable for diffusing drama that I want to mention it again in this context. When someone says words about you that are untrue, or out of context, go to that little seed of truth that led to their perception. As we learned earlier, in everyone's accusation or understanding there is some small seed of truth. Be willing to evaluate that little bit of truth about yourself or your behavior that led to their perception. When we say, "God, show me what in this is true about me," and "Show me what needs to change because of this situation," we are not only being teachable and moldable, but we are humbling ourselves before the Lord so He, and not our defense, can lift us up at the proper time (James 4:10).

Consider It Joy

The Bible tells us, "Consider it all joy, my brethren, when you encounter various trials, knowing that the testing of your faith produces endurance. And let endurance have its perfect result, so that you may be perfect and complete, lacking in nothing" (James 1:2-4 NASB). When we are perfect and complete, lacking in nothing, there is no drama. Do you realize that being perfect and complete, and lacking in nothing, means we are conformed to the image of Christ? That is God's goal for us, isn't it? Can you choose to be content in your circumstances, and even joyful, knowing God is working through them to make you more like His Son?

Final Curtain Call

I suppose if God were to let us see the final scene of our lives

ahead of time, we'd understand where He is going with all that
He allows to happen to us. Then it would be much easier to
trust Him with what we consider "drama." But that is not faith.
Hebrews 11:1 says that faith is the assurance of things *hoped
for,* the conviction of things *not seen.* God has given us enough
evidence in His Word—in the book of Romans alone—that
He loves us (Romans 8:38-39), that He is for us, not against
us (8:31), and that He can work all things in our life for good
(8:28). So trust Him and let go of the drama. Live the adventure
He brings your way, without resistance. And by so doing, you are
not only allowing Him to conform you to the image of His Son,
but you are closing the curtain on unnecessary drama and letting
Him usher you into a new opening act.

A Point to Process

We can close the curtain on our drama when we are convinced of God's track record and ability to do "immeasurably
more than all we ask or imagine" (Ephesians 3:20) with whatever we surrender to Him.

A Truth to Consider

*When the storm is over, there's nothing left of the wicked;
good people, firm on their rock foundation, aren't even fazed.*
PROVERBS 10:25 MSG

A Focus for the Week

Think of someone to whom you can extend forgiveness and
take the initiative.

A Prayer from the Heart

Lord God, I truly want to close the curtain on the small story of my life and be a part of Your greater story. Help me to realize that everything You bring my way is to grow me and develop me into the woman You desire me to be. Forgive me for the times I'm a handful to others because I haven't been resting in Your capable hands and trusting You with all that concerns me. Help me to be a woman who acknowledges Your control in every circumstance of my life, continues to build on You as my firm foundation, and forgives others so no seed of bitterness can form in my heart. Thank You, Lord, that Scripture does not define You as my driftwood—never in the same place twice. And You are not my roller coaster. You are my immovable Rock of Refuge to whom I can always go.[5]

Chapter 10

A New Opening Act

Maintaining a Drama-Free Life

Anyone who belongs to Christ has become a new person.
The old life is gone; a new life has begun!
2 CORINTHIANS 5:17 NLT

I remember the evening I started living a new opening act.

My mother, who had long suffered from chronic back pain, had just had major back surgery. I hadn't heard from her since the surgery, although I texted and left a couple messages—with her *and* my brother, who lived near her and was checking in with her at the hospital. I received a few jumbled text messages from her that made no sense at all, and a call from her cell phone in which no one responded on the other end.

I reminded myself that my brother would call me if there was need for alarm, and that God was engineering the circumstances—even in light of the fact that I was writing a book on being drama free!

Three days after Mom's surgery, I finally heard her voice. But

I could barely tell it was her. She called at 9 p.m. (midnight her time) and struggled to talk, telling me she was in excruciating pain. She said she had been given pain medication, but the doctor wasn't allowing any more of it for several hours. She called to say she didn't think she could make it through the night.

I knew, in that moment, I had a number of choices:

1. I could panic and meet her at the level of her emotions, and then call my brother at midnight to let him know what was going on and chew him out for not responding to the situation. After that, I could make sure my husband and daughter knew the drama I was experiencing with my extended family, thereby escalating the drama in three different locations.

2. I could become angry that she wasn't getting enough medication and demand to speak to a nurse and insist that she get the pain relief she needed. (I learned later that a lack of communication among her three doctors was the reason behind their insistence that she not have any more meds that night, and thus my phone call to a nurse would have had no effect.)

3. I could dismiss her concerns by assuming she was being overly dramatic because women in my family—including myself—can tend to be that way.

4. I could ask God for wisdom in the moment and then talk to her calmly, pray for her, and remind her that God is in control and He would be holding her hand through the night. And instead of losing sleep that night, I could go to bed, pray for her, and know that God would grant her and me peace (Philippians 4:6-7).

I'm so glad I took that last option. I talked in a calm, loving voice, told Mom how badly I felt that she was in such pain, prayed for her, and asked God to "still the storm" and be her peace, provider, protector, and physician through the night.

I also reminded her that God was allowing all this to shape her for His purposes and glorify Himself as she depended on Him during her suffering. (Not everyone needs a reminder or lesson while they are in pain, but I reminded her because I knew it was the deep desire of my mother's heart to glorify God, whatever her circumstance. And that reminder was something that provided comfort to her in the moment.)

My mom calmed down, softly told me she loved me, and hung up the phone. And I did something new. I didn't call each of my siblings and talk of the "drama" I'd just experienced with Mom. I didn't recount the situation to my own family so they'd know all I had gone through. Instead, I thanked the Lord quietly that through His help, Mom was comforted, the two of us were drawn closer together, and the drama was diffused.

As far as it depends on me, I can *be drama free!*

You and I *can* get to a new opening act when it comes to how we handle drama in our lives. We don't have to stay in the same cycle of dysfunction because of how we were raised. We don't have to feel like we're losing our mind with one circumstance after another that overwhelms us. We don't have to lose sleep over what others are saying because we've always had a problem with being misunderstood. We don't even have to continually be excessive stuffers or extreme blowers because of how we were taught to deal with our emotions.

Yes, it's true. We can finally have a new opening act—one in which we die.

A Time to Die

In Galatians 2:20 we read:

> I have been crucified with Christ and I no longer live, but Christ lives in me. The life I now live in the body, I live by faith in the Son of God, who loved me and gave himself for me.

In *The Message*, that verse reads like this:

> Indeed, I have been crucified with Christ. My ego is no longer central. It is no longer important that I appear righteous before you or have your good opinion, and I am no longer driven to impress God. Christ lives in me. The life you see me living is not "mine," but it is lived by faith in the Son of God, who loved me and gave himself for me. I am not going to go back on that.

It's no longer a matter of "I blew it again."
It becomes a matter of "I surrender again."

Do you realize that when we die to our own identity and instead identify with Christ, our emotions are no longer central? Our opinions are not the ruling force. Our perceived rights are not insisted upon. Our emotions, opinions, and rights are His. We belong to Him. He is the One who feels, thinks, and expresses Himself through us. And that means His response becomes our response, and His actions become our actions. It's no longer a matter of "I blew it again." It becomes a matter of "I surrender again." It's a matter of thinking—or saying aloud—*I'm Yours, God, for whatever You have in mind.*

Say this with me: There is no easier way to be drama free than to be free of *me*. Free of self and filled up with the person of Christ.

Jesus said in Luke 9:23, "If anyone wishes to come after Me, he must deny himself, and take up his cross daily and follow Me" (NASB). To take up our cross daily means to forget about ourselves and set aside concerns about self-justification, a spotless reputation, a good "image," and an inconvenience-free life. It means to take on His cause—His cross—in absolute surrender and obedience to our Father.

When the apostle Paul, who had been completely transformed by Christ, addressed the men of Athens and the Greek philosophers in Acts 17:28, he said, "'For in him we live and move and have our being.' As some of your own poets have said, 'We are his offspring.'" Through trusting in Christ alone (and not our own goodness) for our salvation, we become Christ's "offspring"—infused with the character of Christ, not our own dysfunction.

How long have you been a woman who is involved in some sort of drama? How long would you say you've let people or situations take an emotional toll on you? You don't have to be that woman anymore. It's time for a new opening act.

The Bible tells us, "If anyone is in Christ, he is a new creature; the old things passed away; behold, new things have come" (2 Corinthians 5:17 NASB). What does it really mean to be a new creature? It means we are remade, transformed, completely different. It means we have a new focus, a new set of values, and a new set of behaviors.

Corena, a reader of mine who has been a believer for years, sees very clearly the difference between who she used to be emotionally and who she is today after a complete surrender to Christ.

> I don't know if it's just my background or the fact that everyone is just uncertain in life and loses focus on the temporary state of living on earth, but I notice certain factors that cause drama and confusion among most people. It seems like they are throwing a tantrum when life happens and they are not in control.
>
> I have been even-keeled most of my life. I know for certain that walking closer to Jesus gives me grace to remain surprisingly drama free! Most of my drama in the past occurred in my mind. Jesus took over the past six months, and I know with my focus on Jesus it's been much easier to roll with life's punches.

Maybe you can't see your before-and-after emotional state as clearly as Corena because you've been in a relationship with God for quite some time and can't pinpoint when absolute surrender happened. But, like Corena, you should be able to see a difference between the way you responded to a situation six months ago and the way you are responding today.

....

Our response to situations should improve
the more closely we walk with Jesus.

....

In a relationship with Christ, we are either growing or digressing, and how we respond to situations should be something that improves the more closely we walk with Jesus. When we yield control of our lives to the Only One who can control life, we let His character traits (the fruits of the Spirit from Galatians 5:22-23) flow through us so Christ's character and our character become intertwined. *He must increase, and I must decrease.*

Some New Opening Acts

Throughout this book I've shared with you some dramatic moments (or moments that could have led to drama) in many of my friends' lives. Now I want to share with you where some of them are today, as well as others who have experienced God's work in their lives and have found what I call their "new opening act."

A Calm Assurance

Allison, whom you read about in chapter 5, no longer overreacts to situations as she did when her young son crashed his bike. In fact, how she handled a recent situation showed me that this woman is now far from drama.

Upon learning of her husband's colon cancer diagnosis, Allison texted me three drama-free words: *God's got this.* Not a *Why him?* or *Why did God allow this?* Not even a *What if...?* And nothing about how she *felt.* She communicated only a calm assurance that God had the situation under control. That showed me an unswerving trust in the One who can handle all things.

Allison was able to respond that way because she has been a student of the Word of God and is now a teacher of it. That has impacted the way she views and responds to life. The problem-solving skills that she learned from her husband, as well as her ability to trust in God with the help of the Holy Spirit, have transformed her into a woman who no longer focuses on the worst in the situation, but trusts in her God to do the best.

Guy is now in remission, and Allison has been through her own unique set of health problems. But outbursts like "He could've died!" and "I could've been killed!" don't escape her lips anymore. Allison admits she does her share of fretting and has occasional early morning prayer and wrestling sessions with God, "but I'm thankful the habit of my life now is not worry."

"It is human to wonder and speculate, but it doesn't tie me up in knots the way it used to," she said.

Do you want that type of unquestioning faith in the face of uncertainty? Like Allison, do you want to be able to say "God's got this" when the unexpected comes your way? I do. And we have the ability to display that kind of trust in God because we've been given the same thing that Allison has been given: God's trustworthy Word.

God's Word tells us our Father is intimately aware of *all* of our ways and that He knows all our thoughts (and concerns) before we even think them (Psalm 139:1-4). We can be assured that He is already working on the matters that concern us most.

Anytime we find ourselves in a situation we can't do anything about (which is often how life works…and often a contributor to drama), we can trust that God is who He says He is, and that He can work out the situation far better than we can.

The next time you feel like you have to control something, ask yourself: *What am I believing about God that isn't true? Do I believe He is true to His Word? Do I believe He can take care of this?*

When you can answer those questions with the affirming statement, "God's got this," you will experience His peace.

A Greater Awareness

Donna—my friend who suffered the loss of her parents and then faced her own cancer diagnosis—is now a woman who often thinks of others first. "I found out how much people care as I started going through cancer, so now I don't ever want to be too busy for people," she said. "I want to be one of those people who cares when someone else goes through a crisis."

Donna's drama showed her that everyone else deals with some sort of physical pain, heartache, loss, or drama. And she can be oblivious to it if she's focused on herself and her own little world. She wants to instead have eyes open wide to see what people are going through so she can be a part of God's plan to encourage women around her.

A Quiet Trust

Alena, whose story of losing it at the voting booth is in chapter 8, is quite the drama-free woman today. Twelve years to the day of her husband's lymphoma diagnosis, she sat in a doctor's office and received her own diagnosis of a brain tumor. But instead of wigging out, she received the news peacefully. Her mind went immediately to Isaiah 55:8: "'For my thoughts are not your thoughts, neither are your ways my ways,' declares the LORD."

Alena's "new opening act" started that day with what she described as "peace that descended deep into my soul." God changed this feisty woman into a grace-filled woman who carries a presence-of-God peace with her everywhere she goes. Alena has every excuse for a meltdown today (she could just claim that something is wrong with her head—she actually introduced herself to me that way years ago, showing she has kept her sense of humor about her condition). Yet she maintains a peace that God has her life in His hands, and she continues to be a testimony to others of what peace and a quiet trust in God looks like.

Leaving Behind the Dysfunction of Drama

Gayla (from chapter 7) has witnessed God's transformation in the lives of many women who have dealt with difficulties in the past. "Being a pastor's wife for 40 years, I have seen a lot of women deal with drama. Poor reactions to life situations are usually a result of how a woman was raised and how her family taught her to cope," she said. "I have also seen the amazing benefits of a woman becoming stabilized in God. No matter what her background or her experience in life, when a woman surrenders her life to Jesus Christ, she becomes more balanced in her thinking, her processing, and her reactions. It is absolutely the most wonderful transformation to watch!"

...

When a woman surrenders her life to Jesus Christ, she becomes more balanced in her thinking, her processing, and her reactions.

...

Gayla shared the following story with excitement in her voice and a light in her eyes:

We had a lady in our church many years ago who was extremely depressed. She held her head down most of the time. We learned that she had been in psychiatric care for several years and was taking a lot of drugs for her depression. We began to minister to her and encourage her to come to our Bible studies and services.

As the power of the Holy Spirit filled her life, we would literally see changes every week in her countenance. After a year, she looked like a completely different woman! She held her head up, she dressed nicer, she talked with people, and she became very faithful to the church.

After two years, she quit taking all of her

medications and became engaged in social activities. She also received the best job offer of her life. She began tithing and received a large promotion and became the head of a department! Her relationship with her daughters became better. She became a woman who smiled all the time, and people who knew her before could not even recognize her when they saw her. The love of Jesus and her desire to put Him first radically changed the drama of her life!

While this woman's transformation was quite dramatic, it is evidence that God can work in situations where there is much baggage. Can you imagine going from depressed and hopeless to regenerated? It's possible.

I find it interesting that the word *drama* starts with the letter *d* and so does the word *dysfunction* and several other words that describe the results of our dysfunction and the catalysts for our drama:

- disappointment
- discouragement
- disillusionment
- dissension
- despair
- depression
- doubt

And yet God can redeem any situation that causes a *d*, when we surrender ourselves to the Holy Spirit's control. It's interesting that *redeem* starts with *re* and so do many of the results of redemption:

- restoration
- regeneration
- rejuvenation
- renewed perspective
- renewal of our hearts
- refueling
- reenergized life

Your New Opening Act

Every one of us was born into sin, and therefore, sinful behavior and dysfunction is our human nature. But it isn't our nature once we come to know Christ. Christ gives us a new nature when we surrender our lives to the Holy Spirit's control. We can then have the characteristics of Christ rather than the characteristics naturally ingrained in us or learned over the years. As the theologian Lewis Sperry Chafer said, "The new divine nature is more deeply implanted in [our] being than the human nature of [our] earthly father or mother."[1]

That gives me hope. I pray it encourages you too as you enter this new opening act in which God shines through you and takes center stage as you joyfully—yet humbly—fade into the background.

A New Motto

As we started this book together, I had you recite our new motto: *As far as it depends on me, I will be drama free.*

That is the key, isn't it? *As far as it depends on me.* Romans 12:18 instructs: "If it is possible, as far as it depends on you, live at peace with everyone." Because drama always involves another person, that makes you and me the ones who have to make the choice to be drama free. So, as far as it depends on us, let's be drama diffusers (bringing it down a notch), and drama diverters (diverting the focus to Jesus, not us). Quite a bit of the drama in our lives actually does depend on us. It depends on whether or not we enable or allow it to happen, and it depends on how we respond to it. It also depends on who we insist on spotlighting.

So let's vow right now to become women who display the characteristics of Jesus and remain calm in the chaos and at peace when everyone else panics. Let's be the women in the room who respond maturely and diffuse the childish and dramatic outbursts. Let's be advocates of the greater, more meaningful story and please the One who has set His story in our hearts so we can live a life of peace, joy, and no regret.

Oh, how I long to be drama free. Don't you?

Then let's start living our motto: *As far as it depends on me, I will be drama free.*

We can *do* this!

A Point to Process

When we surrender completely to the Lord Jesus, we can have a new opening act—free from the dysfunction of our past—in which He is at center stage and we fade into the background.

Two Truths to Consider

*Whatever you do, work at it with all your heart,
as working for the Lord, not for human masters.*
COLOSSIANS 3:23

God is not working toward a particular finish—His purpose is the process itself. It is the process, not the outcome, that

*is glorifying to God. God's training is for now, not later. His
purpose is for this very minute, not for sometime in the future.
If we realize that moment-by-moment obedience is the goal,
then each moment as it comes is precious.*[2]

OSWALD CHAMBERS

A Focus for the Week

Be aware of every situation in which you start to act unlike
you and more like Christ. Keep a journal or reward yourself with
a snack, treat, or a bit of downtime when you see your emotions
lining up with the Lord's. Leaving your dysfunction behind and
living like a restored, redeemed individual with new emotional
habits and expressions is liberating.

A Prayer from the Heart

*God, may the glorification of Your Son, Jesus, be the
central opening act in my life. And may the world see
Him, not me, through everything I say and do. You must
increase, and I must decrease. You must shine, and I
must fade away. Thank You for the immense privilege
of being a part of Your greater story that elevates Your
Son. May I be free of me and full of Him.*

Drama Queens in the Bible and What We Can Learn from Them

Throughout Scripture, we find many wounded women who became drama queens. These imperfect women—like you and me—responded emotionally and resentfully to their circumstances and created unhealthy drama. These stories—or "cast bios"—can give us insight into the root causes behind *our* drama today.

Which Woman Most Resembles You?

Rachel—the Woman Who Wanted Everything

Rachel, the preferred wife of Jacob (the heir of Abraham and Isaac), had love, wealth, and a promising future in front of her. But Rachel didn't have any children. And she must have thought that having children would be her ticket to having it all!

Being childless, and being jealous of her older sister, Leah, who had several children, sent Rachel into a tailspin with drama that negatively affected her relationship with her husband, her sister, and God. Rachel dramatically and unfairly demanded that her husband give her children or she would die. I'm not kidding. Her exact words were, "Give me children, or else I die!" (Genesis 30:1 NKJV). *Really? Isn't that a bit dramatic, Rachel? Are you really going to die if you don't have children?*

The tragedy is that Rachel eventually had a child, and as soon as he was born, she was pining for another one. A few years later, this woman who said, "Give me children, or else I die" ended up dying in childbirth after delivering her second child (and naming him Ben-Oni, which means "son of my trouble"). Now that is drama with a very tragic ending. (This story is found in Genesis 29:14–30:24 and 35:16-20.)

A Lesson to Learn

How much drama would have been averted if Rachel had not fought against her childlessness with such bitterness but had accepted her role as Aunt Rachel to her sister's many children? Yet you and I can be drama—even today—when we want something badly enough that we try to push ahead of God's perfect timing in order to get it.

What do you want so badly that it has caused drama in your life? Can you surrender that to God and trust His preferred script for your life?

Zipporah—the Woman Who Wanted Her Way, Not God's

Zipporah, the wife of Moses, knew how to make a point— and a scene. I mean, this woman takes the cake when it comes to drama in the Bible. Not only did she make a scene, but it was one of the most shocking, disturbing, and dramatic scenes in Scripture (not to mention confusing to biblical scholars as well). When God confronted Moses for his disobedience (or perhaps his wife's) in failing to circumcise his son (as a sign of obedience to God's covenant), Moses' life was in danger.[1]

Zipporah "took a sharp stone and cut off the foreskin of her son and cast it at Moses' feet, and said, 'Surely, you are a husband of blood to me!'" (Exodus 4:24-26 NKJV). Wow. She apparently made her point and stormed out of the tent. Way to make a scene, Zip! (Could that be where we got the expression "Zip it!" when we are telling someone to keep their mouth shut?) Although Zipporah's action saved her husband's life, she did it with evident disgust.

Some Bible scholars believe that Zipporah, because she was a Midianite, might have been the one who didn't allow the circumcision of their sons because she didn't believe in it. Or perhaps, out of protective mother mode, she refused to allow her husband to perform the procedure.

Sometime after this incident, Moses sent Zipporah and their two sons back to live with her father in Midian. Then Zipporah saw her husband again several months later, after the deliverance of the Israelites from Egypt (Exodus 18:2-3). Was Moses wanting to spare her and his children from the drama of the exodus from Egypt? Is that why he had her stay with her dad for several months? Or was the drama—or the baggage from that horrible night—too much for Zipporah to handle, such that she asked to take the kids and go back to her father's house? We don't know. But I find it interesting that after Zipporah and her father meet up with Moses in Exodus 18, we don't read of her again.

A Lesson to Learn

There is always drama when we choose our way over God's. What might you be insisting upon that is causing drama in your life? Can you give this to God so you can be known, from now on, as the "Woman Who Obeyed God," rather than the "Woman Who Insisted on Her Own Way"?

Delilah—the Woman Who Betrayed Her Lover

Delilah was the tempting seductress who pretended to be in love with Samson in order to sell him out and get rich. Can you imagine? Maybe she liked the idea of being the person who could get—and repeat—information that no one else knew (sound familiar?). Or maybe she lost her morals when seduced by the promise of a boatload of money. Either way, we read her story and we want to proclaim, "That conniving wench!" (You'd think Samson would've been on to her after the *third* time of telling her his so-called "secret" and seeing that she kept betraying his confidence. But then, Samson apparently wasn't playing with a full deck. Or, he just became plain stupid in the presence of this woman.)

Scripture says, "With such nagging she prodded him day after day until he was tired to death. So he told her everything" (Judges 16:16-17). Oh Samson, you fool! Delilah ratted him out again, and this time, she "[put] him to sleep on her lap" so she could be right there, facing him, as the Philistines shaved his head (thereby stripping him of his strength), restrained him, and gouged out his eyes. Then they led him away to prison (Judges 16:17-21).

How could Delilah live with herself after betraying the man who loved and trusted her? She was a schemer, a liar, and a fake. But some women will do anything to get the scoop and then repeat it, no matter who it hurts.

A Lesson to Learn

Do you ever long to know the details about a situation so you can pass it along to someone else, regardless of how that might affect the other person?

Do you know a woman like Delilah? You may need to steer clear of her for the sake of dialing down the drama in your life.

The Root Causes of Drama

From those three women's stories, we learn some of the root causes of drama:

- disappointment
- lack of contentment
- anger
- jealousy
- obsession over something we can't get
- disobedience to God

- frustration
- bitterness
- not submitting to one's husband
- not being able to control one's circumstances
- greed
- desire for attention
- seeking validation

Deep unresolved hurts, including those from our past, can impact how we respond to situations, express our emotions, and ultimately, how we treat others. If you struggle with one or more of the feelings or actions listed above, give it (or them) to God and ask Him for His grace to become a woman who surrenders rather than lives and escalates drama.

Backstage Pass

Exclusive Resources for the Drama-Free Woman

Here's your exclusive material that will give you an up-close experience with being drama free.

Daily Checklist to Being Drama Free

☐ I will spend time with God (in His Word) before spending time with anyone else (Matthew 22:37-38).

☐ I will bring to God what concerns me and receive His peace that comes through prayer (Philippians 4:6-7).

☐ I will guard my lips by choosing words carefully and not saying anything unless it's well timed and builds up the person who needs to hear it (Ephesians 4:29).

☐ I will limit my words and think before I speak (Proverbs 17:27).

☐ I will be okay without having to speak into every situation I hear about (Proverbs 13:3).

☐ I will practice a heart of gratitude by being thankful in *all* things (1 Thessalonians 5:18).

☐ I will forgive any offenses as soon as they come to mind (Ephesians 4:32).

☐ I will give preferential treatment to others. I don't have to be first (Philippians 2:3-4).

☐   I will give priority time today to those closest to me. I will not make them compete with anything or anyone for my attention (Psalm 90:12).

☐   I will pray for the people I don't want to see or be around today because as I pray for them, God will change my heart toward them (Matthew 5:44).

☐   I will not rush in to rescue a person or situation today unless I've asked God about it first and waited upon Him for His leading (Proverbs 2:11).

☐   I will not listen to gossip (Proverbs 20:19).

☐   I will not say anything about anyone that I wouldn't say in their presence (Proverbs 21:23).

☐   I will look at other people more than my phone or electronic device (Proverbs 25:28).

☐   I will take at least a half hour for myself today to rest, refresh, and refuel (Isaiah 28:12).

☐   I will not be overly concerned about my reputation or image or seek to promote myself (James 4:10).

10 Statements to Verbally Diffuse Drama in the Moment

1. Thank you for your concern.

2. It's best if I don't speak about that.

3. I don't understand why God is allowing this, but I trust Him.

4. This isn't about me.

5. This isn't about either of us.

6. This isn't the appropriate time or place.

7. I don't feel comfortable discussing that without him/her here.

8. Thank you for your honesty in expressing how you feel. Now I need time to process this before I respond.

9. Let's look at the facts, not at how we feel.

10. I know it's not ideal, but I'm thankful that _____
   _____.

15 Ways to Dial Down the Drama in Your Life

1. Listen more, talk less (James 1:19).

2. Guard your mouth (Proverbs 13:3; 21:23).

3. Don't speak—or electronically post—quickly. There is always wisdom in waiting (Proverbs 29:20).

4. Address issues wisely, don't avoid (Matthew 18:15).

5. Choose your friends carefully (Proverbs 12:26; 20:19).

6. Don't listen to—or participate in—gossip (Proverbs 16:28; 21:23).

7. Part ways with a rude or brash person (Proverbs 22:10).

8. Dismiss an offense, don't dwell on it (Proverbs 19:11).

9. Fear God, not people (Proverbs 29:25).

10. Stay away from those who anger easily (Proverbs 22:24).

11. Don't play with what can be addictive (Proverbs 23:29-35).

12. Stay out of a quarrel that isn't yours (Proverbs 26:17).

13. Don't jump to conclusions (Proverbs 25:8).

14. Don't sink to someone else's low (Proverbs 26:4).

15. Don't brag, it may backfire (Proverbs 27:1-2).

Study Questions for Individuals or Small Groups

Chapter 1: All the World's a Stage

1. How do you feel about the idea that all the world is a stage?

2. Briefly think about the "stages" or "audiences" that you have in your everyday life.

   What kind of performances have you registered that you are not very proud of?

   What have you learned from those embarrassing performances?

3. In light of the following verses, what hope do you have in terms of what God might say about your worst performances on record?

   2 Corinthians 5:17:

Philippians 1:6:

Romans 8:28-29:

4. Look at the list of fears on pages 31–32. Are there a few that you could add to that list? Write them in the space below.

Now, ask God to replace those fears with a healthy fear of disappointing *Him,* not others. (A great definition of the fear of God is *a wholesome dread of ever displeasing the Lord.*)

5. All the world's a stage, especially if we make much ado about nothing. Choose a verse below to memorize as your slogan when you are tempted to be drama in the heat of the moment:

   John 3:30: *He must become greater; I must become less.*

   Galatians 2:20: *I have been crucified with Christ and I no longer live, but Christ lives in me.*

   James 4:10: *Humble yourselves before the Lord, and he will lift you up.*

Chapter 2: Accepting Your Script

1. What do you believe is at the root of why people struggle with or resist God's script for their lives?

2. Take a few moments to assess your life at this moment. Not who you were as a child. Not where you hope to be one day. But where you are right now. Put a check mark next to the statement below that most closely resembles your script.

(Don't think about which answer would be most spiritual, or which answer you believe you *should* indicate. Rather, think about which is the most honest assessment.)

Right now my life most closely resembles:

☐   A drama in which life happens, good or bad, but I'm trying to see the spiritual lesson in everything and make my life count.

☐   A drama in which I am the main character and every-thing and everyone revolves around my emotions and what kind of day I'm having. It's not pretty, but it's pretty accurate at this point in time.

☐   A comedy in which I have learned to laugh at myself. It seems like I'm in one funny situation after another— some not so funny, but I have to look at them that way to keep my sanity.

☐   A romance in which there are good days and bad days and each chapter is about how I can end up feeling loved and love in return.

☐   A tragedy. It appears to all be going badly, and I'm hop-ing it doesn't actually end this way.

☐   Other:

Now, dream with me a little. Write in the space below a few sentences about what you'd like your life to look like, from this moment on, if you could actually change your script.

3. What are three things you are thankful for in your life right now?

1._____

2._____

3._____

4. What elements of your script would you rather not deal with right now? Be honest and write them out here:

5. What aspect of God's character will you lean on based on what you've written in the space above? (Circle as many as apply.)

- God's ability to work all things for good (Romans 8:28-29)

- God's power (Romans 8:31,37)

- God's love (Romans 8:38-39)

- God's wisdom (James 1:5)

- Other: _____

Now, in the quiet of this moment, give your expectations to God. He knows your heart, your dreams, and your desires. He also knows what is best for you eternally and not just temporally on this earth. Tell Him you trust Him with what He sees that you cannot, and surrender the script to Him. It's His anyway.

Chapter 3: Redefining Your Role

1. How would you define your role right now? (Write it out as if you were describing your character in the production of your life.)

2. If you were writing your own character, who would you want to be in terms of characteristics, not life's circumstances? Write those characteristics below (such as gentle, loving, trusting, sensitive, bold, assertive, firm, independent, and so on).

3. What character traits that you wrote above are possible for you to attain?

4. Read the following passages of Scripture and indicate the godly characteristic that you can attain through a more intimate relationship with Christ:

   Psalm 15: _____

   Proverbs 22:4: _____

   1 Timothy 6:6: _____

   Galatians 5:22-23: _____

5. Which of the "new roles in Christ" mean the most to you (pages 69–70)?

   Which are the most difficult for you to grasp or live out?

6. Do you tend to be one who reacts or explores when you hear of or experience a difficult situation?

7. How can you be more of an explorer of the ways and wonders of God?

8. Which of the steps in CALM (page 76) do you find most challenging?

9. Which would be most helpful to you?

10. How might God want to redefine your role? Example: *God wants to redefine my role from "Stressed Out One Who Tries to Control It All" to "Rested One Who Leans on God to Control It All."*
    God wants to redefine my role from...

    to...

Chapter 4: Casting the Players

1. To better understand the root causes of drama, read "Cast Bios—Drama Queens in the Bible and What We Can Learn from Them" (pages 197–203) Which of the three "drama queens" can you most relate to and why?

2. What new insights did you gain from these stories about the kind of woman you want—or don't want—to be?
    - Rachel taught me:

    - Zipporah showed me:

- Delilah showed me:

3. What insights did you gain from these stories about the kind of women you *don't* want to be around?

4. Do you agree or disagree with this statement? *Drama is helped or hindered by whom we choose to be around.*

   Explain your answer.

5. Which of the "Five Friends Every Woman Needs" (pages 82–85) is the most crucial in your life?

   Why?

   Which of those friends do you still need in your life?

   Pray that God will send a woman into your life who can fill that category (or several of them).

6. Look through the list of "People Who Are Potential Drama" on pages 85–88). Without naming names (that would be gossip!), make a mental list of how many of those people you currently have in your life.

   Do you ever find that *you* are one of those types of people around others? Explain.

7. Read the following verses and record next to each reference the type of friend that verse is encouraging you to be, or stay away from.

Proverbs 10:18-19: _____

Proverbs 11:12: _____

Proverbs 12:17: _____

Proverbs 12:18: _____

Proverbs 15:18: _____

Proverbs 17:9: _____

Proverbs 20:3: _____

Proverbs 20:19: _____

Proverbs 22:24: _____

8. Which of these three steps (pages 90–91) do you most need to work on?

- Hang with God first
- Have a mentor
- Raise your standards on Who You Share Your Time With

Who will hold you accountable to implement those steps in your life?

Chapter 5: Scene Change—No Longer Overreacting

1. Think of an unsettling situation that took you by surprise. How did you fare in light of having—or not having—a plan?

2. Which is most challenging to you when it comes to having a plan for the unexpected?

   • Be a problem solver
   • Be flexible
   • Be focused on the truth, not the "what-ifs"
   • Be balanced with wisdom from the Word

3. Read Galatians 5:19-23. What characteristics from that list describe you when someone knowingly or unknowingly offends you?

4. Which one or two fruits of the Spirit (Galatians 5:22-23) will you focus on this week?

   _____

   _____

   List one practical way you will practice that (or those) characteristic(s):

5. How are you at staying "hidden" during the drama of an unexpected event or an unexpected offense?

6. Think of a time when one or more of the following helped diffuse drama when you were offended by someone:
   You realized there was more to the story.

You retained a sense of humor.

You refrained from acting impulsively.

You resisted the urge to defend yourself.

7. Read Ephesians 4:29-32 and list every piece of advice that passage gives on how we should respond when we are offended:

8. In addition, what do these verses say about how we should respond when offended?
Exodus 14:14:

Proverbs 12:16:

James 1:19:

James 4:10:

9. Which of the responses listed above will you focus on this week?

Chapter 6: Scene Change—No Longer Overwhelmed

1. What is your natural response when you feel overwhelmed?

2. Read each verse and indicate next to each reference how Scripture commands us to respond when we're feeling overwhelmed:

   Proverbs 3:5-6:

   Proverbs 12:15:

   Proverbs 16:32:

   Philippians 4:6-7:

   Philippians 4:8-9:

3. Read Psalm 42:5-11. Think of a situation that makes you feel stressed or overwhelmed.

4. Read Psalm 71. What do you need to be saved from on a daily basis (an attitude you struggle with, a habit you're trying to drop, a sin you wrestle with, etc.)?

Chapter 7: Scene Change—No Longer Overextended

1. In what ways do you feel overextended right now?

2. Write out everything you do in a typical week. Now, rank these tasks in order of importance, giving numbers 1, 2, and 3 to the things that only *you* can do (assign higher numbers to things that aren't as vital). Take this list to God and ask Him what can be delegated and what can be trimmed from your schedule altogether.

3. Considering the three questions to help you find your focus (page 139), what do you feel God has truly called you to do?

4. Read the following verses and on the line next to them, indicate the priority that the verse is suggesting or commanding:

   Psalm 62:5: _____

   Ecclesiastes 5:18-19: _____

   Matthew 22:37-38: _____

   Matthew 22:39: _____

   Ephesians 5:22,33: _____

   Ephesians 6:1-3: _____

   1 Thessalonians 5:16-18: _____

5. Which of the steps under "Take an Intermission" (pages 140–142) are the most challenging for you? Write them out here. Put an asterisk (*) next to the one you will focus on this week.

Chapter 8: Scene Change—No Longer Self-Absorbed

1. Can you recall making a comment or doing something that unintentionally triggered a dramatic emotional reaction in someone else? How did you handle the situation?

2. Which one of the following "Steps to Being Selfless" (pages 154–155) would be most helpful to you right now and why?

   Consider the other person above yourself

   Consider your words carefully

   Choose to be a listener

3. Think of one practical way that you can practice each of the above steps and write them in the space below.

4. List how you can incorporate the following three steps into a situation that is causing you drama right now:

   Take a breather

Take an inventory

Take it to God

5. Read the following verses and note, briefly, how each can help you be more others-focused:
   Matthew 5:11-12:

   1 Corinthians 13:4-8:

   Galatians 2:20:

   Galatians 5:22-23:

   Ephesians 4:29:

   Ephesians 4:32:

   Philippians 2:3-4:

   Philippians 4:5:

Chapter 9: Closing the Curtain

1. If you could eliminate one thing in order to rid your life of drama, what would that one thing be?

2. We often think eliminating circumstances from our lives (or difficult people) is the answer to a drama-free life. But the answer lies in acknowledging God's control of our script, considering His track record of faithfulness to work it all out for our best, and cultivating a heart of forgiveness.

   We can see these lessons strongly woven through the Old Testament story of Joseph. Read his story in Genesis chapters 37 and 39–50. (This is a long read but an exciting story with a glorious end!) As you read, record the events in the appropriate categories below, as a visual reminder to you of God's track record of faithfulness:

   Reasons for Joseph to Complain of the Drama:

   Evidence of God's presence in—and control of—Joseph's script:

   Evidence of Joseph's trust in God:

   Benefits of Joseph's trust in God:

3. Is there someone you still need to forgive? If so, pray right now that God will help you give that area of offense to Him and

release your offender so you can start living more freely. (For a clearer understanding of what is involved in forgiving someone, see my blog: "Should You Forgive Someone Who Isn't Sorry?" at http://strengthforthesoul.com/2015/08/should-you-forgive-someone-who-isnt-sorry/ or enter "forgive" in the search field on my blog page at www.StrengthForThe Soul.com.)

Chapter 10: A New Opening Act

1. Do you have a new "opening act" by now? If so, describe a situation in which you reacted differently and showed evidence of being a drama-free woman.

2. Read Galatians 2:20. What are the characteristics, personality traits, old ways, or old habits you have "died" to now that you've surrendered your life to Christ? What characteristics now represent the new you? List them in the appropriate sections below. (My answers are in italics to give you some examples.)

The Old Me:
Cindi was controlling, jealous, critical, insecure, and therefore, competitive.

The New Me:
Cindi is now aware of her inability to control things, and she is dependent on Christ, trusting of others, optimistic, confident, and secure in who she is in Christ.

3. Look at the list of *d* words on page 193 that are the results of dysfunction and the catalysts for drama. List the ones here that you struggle—or used to struggle—with.

4. Now look through the *re* words on page 194. Which of these words describe your condition—or the condition you'd like to have—as a result of this study?

5. Read the following verses and record next to the reference the "new creation" you can be through Christ:

   Philippians 2:14-15:

   Colossians 3:15:

   Colossians 4:2:

   1 Thessalonians 5:16:

   1 Thessalonians 5:17:

   1 Thessalonians 5:18:

   2 Timothy 1:7:

James 4:10:

6. Select one of the resources from the Backstage Pass section
   on pages 205–212 to download free from my website (www
   .StrengthForTheSoul.com) so you can tape it on your desk or
   refrigerator, or carry it with you, as a daily reminder of how
   you can be drama free.

An Invitation to Write

How has God helped you through this book? I would love to hear from you and encourage you, personally, and pray for you as well.

You can find me online at www.StrengthForTheSoul.com. Leave me a message that you were there and let me know how I can pray for you. I always respond to my readers.

You can also connect with me on Facebook at Strength for the Soul.

Or you can send me a letter at:

Cindi McMenamin
c/o Harvest House Publishers
990 Owen Loop North
Eugene, OR 97402

To contact me to speak to your group, email me at:
Cindi@StrengthForTheSoul.com

Notes

Chapter 1: All the World's a Stage

1. "Fear of Public Speaking Statistics," Statistic Brain, from a study by the National Institute of Mental Health, September 3, 2016, http://www.statistic brain.com/fear-of-public-speaking-statistics/.

2. This discourse of Jesus is found in Matthew 23:1-28.

3. Oswald Chambers, *My Utmost for His Highest*, ed. James Reimann (Grand Rapids, MI: Discovery House, 1992), November 1.

4. Edward T. Welch, *When People Are Big and God Is Small* (Phillipsburg, NJ: P&R Publishing Company, 1997), 17.

5. *The Message*, by Eugene Peterson, is a translation of the original language of the Bible into idiomatic English, which means it is characteristic of, or in keeping with, the way a language is ordinarily and naturally used by its native speakers. In other words, if the people of the Bible were around today, this is how they would sound. *The Message* is a personal favorite of mine, not for biblical word studies, of course, but for overall thought, application, and context. I especially appreciate how it refreshes and rejuvenates my devotional reading, by bringing fresh insights to a verse I've read multiple times but never understood in today's context.

Chapter 3: Redefining Your Role

1. *Wikipedia*, s.v. "Hurricane Sandy," last modified November 2, 2016, http://en.wikipedia.org/wiki/Hurricane_Sandy.

2. This list was originally published in my book *When a Woman Overcomes Life's Hurts* (Eugene, OR: Harvest House Publishers, 2012), 98–99.

3. Chambers, *My Utmost for His Highest*, July 16.

Chapter 4: Casting the Players

1. *Letting God Meet Your Emotional Needs* can be found at my website: www.StrengthForTheSoul.com. Use the coupon code "dramafree" and receive a $3 discount toward the purchase of this book—an exclusive offer for my readers of *Drama Free*.

2. Henry Blackaby, *Holiness: God's Plan for Fullness of Life* (Nashville: Thomas Nelson, 2003), 80.

Chapter 5: Scene Change—No Longer Overreacting

1. Chambers, *My Utmost for His Highest*, October 21.
2. Richard J. Foster, *Celebration of Discipline* (New York: Harper San Francisco, 1998), 101.

Chapter 7: Scene Change—No Longer Overextended

1. Chambers, *My Utmost for His Highest*, March 24.
2. For more on the concept of burnout, see my book *When You're Running on Empty: Hope and Help for the Overscheduled Woman*. You can read more about it at my website, www.StrengthForTheSoul.com.
3. Chambers, *My Utmost for His Highest*, October 19.

Chapter 8: Scene Change—No Longer Self-Absorbed

1. Susan Silk and Barry Goldman, "How Not to Say the Wrong Thing," *Los Angeles Times*, April 7, 2013, http://articles.latimes.com/2013/apr/07/opinion/la-oe-0407-silk-ring-theory-20130407.
2. Lysa TerKeurst, *Unglued* (Grand Rapids, MI: Zondervan, 2012), 77.

Chapter 9: Closing the Curtain

1. Rhonda Stoppe is the author of *Moms Raising Sons to be Men* and *If My Husband Would Change, I'd be Happy (and Other Myths Wives Believe)*, both published by Harvest House Publishers. You can find out more about Rhonda at www.rhondastoppe.com.
2. Rhonda Stoppe, *Moms Raising Sons to be Men* (Eugene, OR: Harvest House Publishers, 2012), 48.
3. Ibid., 50.
4. You can find this blog post by entering "forgive" in the search field on my blog, or by going directly to this link: http://strengthforthesoul.com/2016/09/why-is-it-so-difficult-to-forgive/.
5. Cindi McMenamin, *God's Whispers to a Woman's Heart* (Eugene, OR: Harvest House Publishers, 2014), 160.

Chapter 10: A New Opening Act

1. Lewis Sperry Chafer, *He That Is Spiritual* (Grand Rapids, MI: Zondervan, 1967), 32.

2. Chambers, *My Utmost for His Highest*, July 28.

Cast Bios

1. In Genesis 17:7-14, God commanded the circumcision of every male among the Israelites, and all their male descendants, as a sign of the covenant between God and His people. God was about to kill Moses because he had not circumcised his own son, and therefore Moses could go no further in God's plan as deliverer of the Israelites from Egypt until Moses fulfilled God's covenant completely.

When Women Walk Alone

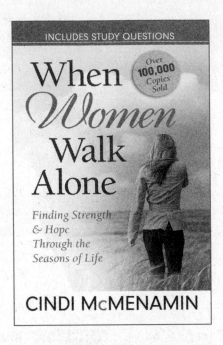

More and more women are finding themselves alone in their Christian walk because of life's circumstances—a lack of support from people in their home, work, or church; being left out of the things they used to be included in; being misunderstood and unable to explain. Cindi McMenamin, author of *Heart Hunger*, offers encouragement and practical, biblical steps for gaining strength in times of isolation and becoming resilient to, not resentful toward, loneliness.

When Women Walk Alone encourages women to see alone times as unique opportunities for personal and spiritual growth.

Other Books by Cindi McMenamin

10 Secrets to Becoming a Worry-Free Mom
(paperback and ebook)

When a Woman Discovers Her Dream
(ebook and print on demand)

Letting God Meet Your Emotional Needs
(ebook and print on demand)

When You're Running on Empty
(ebook and print on demand)

When God Sees Your Tears
(paperback and ebook)

Women on the Edge
(ebook and print on demand)

When Women Long for Rest
(ebook and print on demand)

When a Woman Overcomes Life's Hurts
(paperback and ebook)

To learn more about Harvest House books and
to read sample chapters, visit our website:

www.harvesthousepublishers.com

HARVEST HOUSE PUBLISHERS
EUGENE, OREGON